Auditing Beyond Compliance

Also available from ASQ Quality Press:

The ASQ Auditing Handbook, Third Edition
J.P. Russell, editing director

Quality Audits for Improved Performance, Third Edition
Dennis R. Arter

The Internal Auditing Pocket Guide: Preparing, Performing, Reporting and Follow-up, Second Edition
J.P. Russell

Process Driven Comprehensive Auditing: A New Way to Conduct ISO 9001:2008 Internal Audits, Second Edition
Paul C. Palmes

AS9101D Auditing for Process Performance: Combining Conformance and Effectiveness to Meet Customer Satisfaction
Chad Kymal

Lean Acres: A Tale of Strategic Innovation and Improvement in a Farm-iliar Setting
Jim Bowie

Lean ISO 9001: Adding Spark to your ISO 9001 QMS and Sustainability to your Lean Efforts
Mike Micklewright

The Quality Toolbox, Second Edition
Nancy R. Tague

Mapping Work Processes, Second Edition
Bjørn Andersen, Tom Fagerhaug, Bjørnar Henriksen, and Lars E. Onsøyen

Root Cause Analysis: Simplified Tools and Techniques, Second Edition
Bjørn Andersen and Tom Fagerhaug

The Certified Manager of Quality/Organizational Excellence Handbook, Third Edition
Russell T. Westcott, editor

To request a complimentary catalog of ASQ Quality Press publications, call 800-248-1946, or visit our Web site at http://www.asq.org/quality-press.

Auditing Beyond Compliance

Using the Portable Universal Quality Lean Concept

Janet Bautista Smith
ASQ/GE LSS Black Belt, CQA, CQE, CQM

ASQ Quality Press
Milwaukee, Wisconsin

American Society for Quality, Quality Press, Milwaukee, WI 53203
 Published 2012.
Printed in the United States of America.

18 17 16 15 14 5 4 3 2

Library of Congress Cataloging-in-Publication Data

Bautista Smith, Janet
Auditing beyond compliance: using the portable universal quality lean audit model
Janet Bautista Smith.
p. cm.
Includes bibliographical references and index.
ISBN 978-0-87389-840-9 (hardcover : alk. paper)
1. Auditing. I. Title.
HF5667.B268 2012
657'.45—dc23
2012013441

Publisher: William A. Tony
Acquisitions Editor: Matt T. Meinholz
Project Editor: Paul Daniel O'Mara
Production Administrator: Randall Benson

ASQ Mission: The American Society for Quality advances individual, organizational, and community excellence worldwide through learning, quality improvement, and knowledge exchange.

 Printed on acid-free paper

Quality Press
600 N. Plankinton Ave.
Milwaukee, WI 53203-2914
E-mail: authors@asq.org
The Global Voice of Quality™

Dedication

This book is lovingly dedicated to
my son Daniel,
my husband Chet,
my father Ben,
and my nephew Nathan.

Contents

List of Figures and Tables

Preface

Due to many variables, some beyond the auditor's control, audits are not typically perceived as a catalyst for innovation and a driver of growth. Audits are historically dreaded and viewed as an ogre whose main role is to dig up and report errors and imperfections. This may sound like an exaggeration, but it is not too far from the perception most people have of the audit function. Some even consider this function a necessary evil.

Why do we have such a negative attitude toward audits and how can we change this image to highlight the prestige deserved by the audit function?

One culprit is the predictive methodology used by the majority of our internal audit professionals, which tends to advocate compliance verification as a stand-alone, primary audit element. This is the "police ticketing" style of auditing. It tends to isolate clean-up (containment) and corrective action for continuous improvement as the sole responsibilities of the auditees under the shield of "conflict of interest" if auditors are involved. This shield is misunderstood and misused in the world of auditing, creating a silo and branding the audit program as the "outsider."

The second culprit is the audit function's lack of exposure to or first-hand experience with tools, other than traditional compliance verification tools, that could be used to change this negative image. This traditional style is a popular method; it is a "comfort zone" relied upon by many audit practitioners. This style often limits the scope of the audit function to that of a mere "verifier" and a "police patrol," rather than allowing the audit to be a partner in growth and innovation.

Multiple tools and strategies are available to address this image and turn this challenge into a positive initiative. The following chapters, strategies, and models promote a new status that the audit function deserves, such as operations' partner to ensure compliance and a supporter of continuous improvement for the overall success of the system. This is a common dilemma: some quality practitioners perceive that these two paths, compliance and improvement, cannot coexist efficiently and effectively under a shared goal. Various tools can address this challenge; this publication has selected Lean-Six Sigma principles as the primary roadmap to lead the audit program down the path of operational excellence and growth.

Must one be a Lean-Six Sigma Black Belt to deploy Lean-Six Sigma audit methodology? No. This is a myth that often hinders the wide adoption of this philosophy. One can choose the degree of simplicity or complexity of the concept and tools to be used. It is mostly common sense and basic quality tools in action!

PORTABLE AUDIT MODEL

This publication introduces a portable audit model to facilitate a simple, flexible, and effective audit of single or multiple quality system standards to achieve both compliance and initiation of improvement initiatives. This model is similar to a universal adaptor plug, allowing easy connection and interchangeability of the multiple standards even under rapid system changes typical of modern day operations. This universal plug will allow focus on compliance verification and improvement at a high level of consistency with minimum process disruption and cost.

BENEFITS OF THE PORTABLE AUDIT MODEL

Simplification of Audit System

It is not unusual for a company to invest in multiple quality systems certifications (such as ISO 9001, TS 16949, AS9100, TL 9000, CTPAT, industry regulations, and so on) to achieve a competitive edge or satisfy customer requirements. In most cases, customer-specific regulations embedded in the quality system mandated by the customer contract govern a system. This can be a nightmare in disguise if not properly managed to simultaneously deliver full compliance to these multiple regulatory requirements and maintain ongoing operational changes for long-term profitability. The following chapters will demonstrate that the portable audit model introduced in this publication will be a key element in validating the effectiveness of multiple variables if used as an audit template or a detection tool for changes and improvement opportunities. It is comparable to a master key that can replace multiple key sets to achieve the same functionality in a simplified form.

Conversion of Audit Function into Improvement Tool

This publication will provide a universal roadmap that serves as the "converter" in unifying multiple quality elements into a single focal point toward operational excellence and continuous improvement.

Measurement of Audit's Effectiveness

This publication will demonstrate easy steps to design a simple audit program with quantifiable measurement of effectiveness and added value to stakeholders. Effectiveness without measurement is not easily validated and recognized. This is one of the most difficult phases of the audit program action plans. Under the traditional audit method, the mere presence of an action plan may suffice as verification of completion. Under the Lean-Six Sigma methodology, verification includes measurement of effectiveness using appropriate benchmark and metrics.

ADDITIONAL FEATURES OF THIS BOOK

Scope Coverage

Emphasis is not only on compliance but also on improvement of partnership with operations through the use of strategy models. These strategy models will help accentuate the internal audit role as a dynamic element and catalyst for improvement.

Ease of Application

Real life-based challenges (masked identity) are used in case studies to demonstrate the application of typical internal audit methodologies combined with an implementation engine such as Lean auditing strategies. This will clarify theories that are commonly viewed as abstract by the novice and, in some cases, misunderstood by experienced professionals.

Added Value

The universal and portable quality program model introduced in this publication illustrates an efficient and effective application on single or multiple quality certifications. Application of this model is shown in case studies including deployment, verification, and measurement methodologies via internal audit.

This is the breakthrough from a dormant internal audit program into a proactive tool for added-value improvement. Lean methodology is integrated through simple models that don't require one to be a Lean or Black Belt guru. The focus is using logical sense to understand and apply the concept.

Acknowledgements

Special acknowledgement to the Palma family: Noel, Vangie, Nicole, Samantha, Patrick, Donna and Emmanuel Jacob; my sister Jennifer and her son Vincent. Special thanks to Tyang Doring for her encouragement.

I would also like to express my deepest appreciation to ASQ management and Quality Press staff for their hard work, professionalism, and excellent support throughout the different publication phases of this book.

1

Auditing Beyond Compliance Model

Compliance verification is the traditional focus of internal auditing, often overshadowing other elements of the business hierarchy. This outlook has been the historical audit pattern, although deep within the system there is a natural tendency to question this conventional wisdom because the world of auditing is continually evolving beyond compliance. During the recent unpredictable economy, this direction has been seen to be a logical path to growth and profitability. Compliance alone will not achieve quality sustainability or operational competitiveness in our dynamic environment. As a matter of fact *compliance,* if deployed as a stand-alone element, is static and likely to act as a deterrent to progress; in some cases it may act as a barrier, unyielding to innovation and growth. What is the reason for this inflexibility?

The customary rigid compliance approach to auditing may have originated from human nature's tendency to succumb to the path of least complexity, such as the desire to function in the comfort zone. It is sometimes easier to block the flow of new or nontraditional methodologies than it is to understand them. When embarking on a journey with a new or unknown concept, fear of failure may be one reason for resistance to change. Compliance verification is the traditional audit, a "black and white" comparison against the standard requirements that is simple to deploy. It is true that compliance is a major element in customer satisfaction. However, compliance alone lacks the vigor to drive dynamic change for growth. The goal of this publication is to enhance the effectiveness and added value of compliance auditing through the incorporation of an implementation engine such as the Lean-Six Sigma (LSS) methods to drive improvement.

The traditional audit path is often myopic; this is a common weakness that can be easily addressed if its existence is first recognized and acknowledged so efforts can be rerouted to a more dynamic path. This path diversion is quite simple but will require commitment and perseverance in understanding and applying the appropriate tools, as well as making adjustments along the way.

Figure 1.1 depicts the key steps for an effective strategy in the application of this Audit Beyond Compliance model.

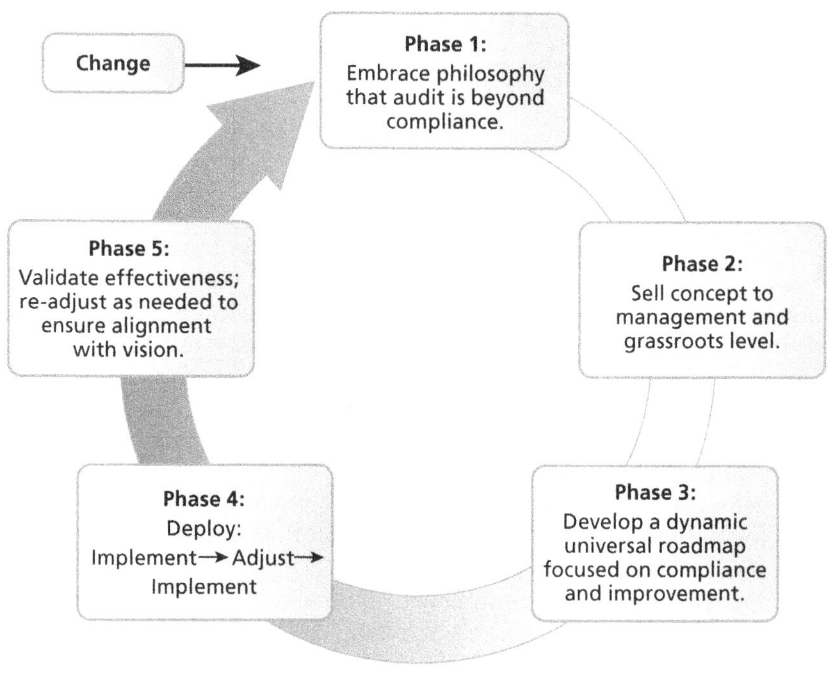

Figure 1.1 Audit Beyond Compliance model.

Phase 1 – Embrace Philosophy that Auditing is Beyond Compliance

The audit management needs to understand and embrace the philosophy that auditing is beyond compliance and that auditing is also a powerful tool and catalyst for change and improvement. This philosophy may be a cultural shock to certain branches of the audit function with exposure limited solely to compliance verification. Once this concept is understood, appreciated, and adopted, it will be easier to advocate to the rest of the organization. The acceptance of the concept is one of the major steps the audit function must undertake before this program cycle can truly begin.

Phase 2 – Sell Concept to Management and the Grassroots Level

Once the audit function has fully accepted Phase 1, the next step is to champion the selling of this concept to management and the grassroots level and secure buy-in on the audit focus: compliance and growth. Superficial acceptance of this concept alone will not generate success; there must be commitment and an embrace of the program in order to sustain the initiative's longevity. Change must occur from within if it is to be self-sustaining. Forced change is only implemented through policing; when policing stops, the system goes back to the old ways. Grassroots acceptance and visible management support will keep the program moving with the system flow. What are some of the selling points, other than improvement and possible savings?

- Streamlining work by reducing waste will help the workforce be more productive.
- Stronger team effort and participation in initiatives will replace silos within the system; silos create discontent and unproductive behavior.
- Involving process owners and subject experts in growth initiatives rather than making them the "fall guy" for system errors will empower the workforce.

Phase 3 – Develop a Dynamic Universal Roadmap Focused on Compliance and Improvement

Development of simple strategies to initiate and sustain Phases 1 and 2 is critical in keeping a sustained deployment. Lean-Six Sigma (LSS) is one tool that can help accomplish this goal. LSS is not the only tool; users can select from an array of available tools compatible with the user's system. Sometimes complex problems are solved with simple ideas and tools. The chosen toolkit must generate results aligned with the company vision and provide measurable and achievable goals.

The design of this dynamic and universal tool may not be achieved during the first try—it may take several changes before it can be deployed. Just as with any other system change, this tool must be verified to ensure its compatibility with the users and the business direction. In some cases, the verification of effectiveness can be done in selected segments of the business before a full release; in this way, the tool can be adjusted and re-adjusted with minimum disruption to the routine process.

Phase 4 – Deploy: Implement → Adjust → Implement

Implementation of the program does not mean the cycle has been completed. Some elements not identified during the pre-deployment phase may surface during implementation and create unanticipated "speedbumps." Adjustments may be needed to address these bumps and create a smooth process flow. Several adjustments may be needed before an acceptable result is achieved; thus measurable parameters are necessary to baseline these adjustments.

Phase 5 – Validate Effectiveness; Re-adjust as Needed

Continue validating and readjusting Phase 3; this is a "perpetual circle of growth." The Audit Beyond Compliance model is a continuous circle with elements that may change at any time, a characteristic typical of robust processes; elements in motion mean a dynamic quality program. Typically, change occurs when the model reaches maturity. However, it should be anticipated that change could occur at any phase of the cycle, initiated by the interaction of internal processes and external (that is, customer- or industry-driven) catalysts. If the system is designed with built-in flexibility, change will cause minimum disruption to process equilibrium. This flexibility is key to breaking the mode of dormancy associated with the myopic approach to compliance auditing. The milestones are the catalyst to maintaining a continuous cycle of improvement initiatives. Without these change agents, the program will remain stagnant, just like a dormant pond where there is no water movement to refresh the system.

These phases of the Audit Beyond Compliance model can be viewed as leverage tools for identifying opportunities aligned with the company vision and customer expectations. This alignment is crucial in the strengthening of the audit program's role in the system, often invisible to the rest of the business. This role is the championship of improvement and customer satisfaction by auditing beyond compliance.

2

Advocate the Philosophy

HOW DO YOU AUDIT BEYOND COMPLIANCE?

Compliance is just one element of auditing. It has financial and sometimes legal ramifications and impact on customer satisfaction, and it is not optional. However, if left in a static mode, compliance alone may not sustain the business and the system may start to deteriorate. The system is like a sailboat driven forward by the sail (such as compliance). To maintain a dynamic flow, the boat needs a consistent wind stream to reach its destination. Just like the wind stream, improvement and growth act as the dynamic boost to continue that journey to success. Change is a key catalyst that is likely to promote growth if managed in the right direction. Endorsement of change does not have to be a complex matter; it can be as simple as identification of wastes and basic improvement opportunities uncovered during the audit activities. This strategy sounds simple, yet many auditors miss this opportunity. Why?

The following are possible major culprits:

- Auditing functions are deployed under a traditional mode of compliance verification, historically perceived as "police enforcement with no or little visible added value." We must break this constraint and enhance the audit function's image as it partners with operations in improvement initiatives. The audit function can maintain independence (remain unbiased) as an audit entity and yet champion improvement changes. Some company structures have separate audit and improvement functions and this may appear to be a roadblock to the auditing beyond compliance strategy. This is not the case—the audit function, structurally independent or combined with improvement teams (engineering, LSS, and so on), has the opportunity to partake in improvement initiatives. This is like being in the observation tower, able to see all activities and "zoom in" on crucial areas as needed. The audit function's access to the different business segments can be a great leverage in identifying compliance and improvement opportunities most often hidden underneath process noise. Uncovering this vital information during audits is a crucial step in the initiation of a continuous improvement "awakening."

- Failure to understand the measurable benefits of audit beyond compliance is a roadblock in the effort to deviate from the traditional "compliance police" image. Compliance through the policing method is actually more difficult to sustain because the audit function carries the burden of perception; auditors are seen only as the catchers of "violators." This expectation is difficult to maintain. Most auditing is based on sampling; in most cases, auditing or inspection is not 100% reliable. Auditing in this environment may be more expensive in the long run because to maintain quality performance based on policing is only effective while policing; non-compliance tends to come back when there is no enforcer.

  This burden of the invisible police badge can actually be transformed into self-motivated compliance of the process owners with visible accountability. How? The auditing beyond compliance strategy championed by this publication identifies tools used for reporting measurable audit findings (such as cost of lost opportunity, wasted resources, or measurable savings) that will likely attract the attention and support of a wider audience including management.

- An audit program lacks a model for easy recognition of waste and improvement opportunities because these variables are oftentimes camouflaged by process noise. The following chapters show the positive results of augmenting the conventional audit style with application engines such as Lean-Six Sigma to eliminate this roadblock.

- Improvement opportunities are often missed due to the short-sightedness of the audit roadmap, which highlights compliance as the only key variable. There are many routes to achieving auditing beyond compliance. Just as with freeway maps, there are multiple entry and exit points en route to a certain destination. The selection of the best route is affected by many variables depending on the traveler's agenda: available time, preferred driving speed, preference for scenic views, and so on. Similarly, there are various options for designing a simple, cost-efficient internal audit roadmap leading to the desired destination. The selection is dependent on the company's vision, business plan, and prevailing regulatory requirements.

HOW DO YOU ADVOCATE THE PHILOSOPHY OF AUDITING BEYOND COMPLIANCE?

Auditing may be executed in various ways under different names such as gap analysis, self-check, process walk, product audit, process audit, and so on. Regardless of the name, auditing beyond compliance requires, at minimum, verifiable or measurable goals and expected results.

A typical audit report, if no adverse finding was found, may state something like this:

> *"No discrepancy noted; system showed evidence of compliance with elements x, y, z; sampled record a, b, c as evidence..."*

It is good, of course, that the system was found in compliance, but this result did not offer added valued to stakeholders with regard to growth and continuous improvement. Quality practitioners or audit management can optimize the effectiveness of the audit function if the audit provides measurable observations of the current status, in comparison with stakeholder expectations. If expectations are not met, then the existence of the gap must be identified for further data mining and analysis. The data mining may be performed not necessarily by the auditor but by the process owners, and verification of results may be part of the audit follow-up on the status of the action plan. This is an initiation of an improvement opportunity, breaking the passive state of the audit event. Some auditors will find auditing beyond compliance a "foreign territory" for a short period of time, because there is always a learning curve for change. Once the tools for the execution of this method are understood, this strategy will be more appreciated because it will bring the audit function into a favorable light. The audit function is now a partner in growth, not just for compliance.

Auditing beyond compliance means verifying compliance against a standard that includes the measurement of critical metrics associated with process or system performance against expected results. This method is geared to analyze both input and output variables affecting the gap between actual performances and expectations.

These examples differentiate this audit style from the typical audit focused solely on compliance:

- **Recognition of hidden costs that may affect customer satisfaction.** Hidden costs can be identified if auditors are cognizant of the basic cost drivers associated with the product, process, or system being audited. An old saying may have some application for this purpose: *"Follow where the money goes and you will find the culprit."* Some companies provide audit teams with subject expertise pertinent to the audit subject. A finance representative may be included in the audit team as a "subject expert" if the audit will delve into finance issues.

- **Identification of "hidden factories" or silos within the system** that are not visible but that have negative impact (for example, rework data not captured or over-qualified skill set performing non-critical tasks to achieve immediate personal glory). These represent an ineffective quality system with poor resource allocation and planning.
- **Identification of wastes causing roadblocks to efficiency.** Wastes such as redundant processing, excessive material handling, and unnecessary motion can cause errors and inappropriate allocation of valuable resource needed to achieve customer satisfaction. Fatigue, for example, is known to cause accidents or errors. Identifying unnecessary wastes causing fatigue will not only save time or resources, it could also save lives.
- **Understanding the process/system being audited to identify bottlenecks.** This may not solve the issues immediately, but it will allow process owners to identify root causes and develop action plans. Bottlenecks (delays causing late deliveries, overtime due to extended processing, errors due to fatigue) affect stakeholders and ultimately affect customer satisfaction.
- **Identification of improvement opportunities.** These can be detected through the review of performance metrics such as capacity versus productivity index, cycle time, on-time delivery, and complaint trends. In some cases, improvement opportunities are signaled by seemingly remote and unrelated events. These are the hidden treasures that may be uncovered through auditing beyond compliance. Keen observation of the environment and basic common sense will be some of the strongest tools for this initiative.
- **Recognition of waste impacting process.** Is data collection effective? Does the company use valuable resources to collect metrics and then do nothing with the information to initiate improvement? This is not just waste of valuable resource but also a hindrance to an efficient process flow, without a justifiable return of investment.

The goal is to question or recognize trends or other signs of process fluctuation or system distress; auditing beyond compliance does not necessarily mean solving issues as they are discovered during the audit. These observations should be assigned appropriately for further evaluation and should be verified during the follow-up audit.

WHAT TOOLS WILL LEAD TO THESE DISCOVERIES DURING AUDITING BEYOND COMPLIANCE?

One with limited experience and knowledge of Lean-Six Sigma (LSS) may find it challenging to integrate this application engine with the typical audit method, at least during the start-up phase. As with any set of tools, the choice is dependent on the need or expected results. One would not use a bulldozer to plant a small shrub; a simple shovel would be more appropriate. However, if the project involves planting thousands of shrubs in a park setting, then a ride-on post digger may be more appropriate, especially if project time constraints and manpower costs would justify purchase of the post digger. The LSS tool selection has the same philosophy. In the beginning it will be practical to use simple tools; simple tools are always advantageous in analyzing and interpreting data. The good news: there are many simple LSS tools available that are easy to understand with flexible application. But if this is true, why are LSS tools not widely used in auditing? As mentioned earlier, the comfort zone of auditing includes the use of traditional compliance verification. With the changing economy and steep market competition, companies relying solely on compliance may not survive the fierce race for growth. It is to the audit function's benefit to have a built-in mechanism for involvement in the improvement and growth of the system through auditing beyond compliance.

Table 2.1 Examples of auditing beyond compliance.

Conventional audit finding	Auditing beyond compliance (measurable metrics to evaluate success included)
Example 1: **No system or procedure to prevent potential line mix up**	
Verification of action plan: Procedure has been modified to include line clearance to prevent part number mix-up and implemented as of (date). **Closed.**	Verification of action plan: Procedure has been modified to include line clearance to prevent part number mix-up and implemented as of (date). The following records were verified as evidence of effectiveness. • **Error rate** of mixing part numbers is zero from xx to xx – no discrepancy noted. • **Line clearance log** indicates frequency difference between the 2nd and 3rd shifts; recommended manager's evaluation; auditor to follow up in 2 weeks. • **Waiting time:** Operators were observed waiting for 30 minutes for completion of line clearance inspection; recommended manager's evaluation of schedule to reduce waiting time; auditor to follow up in 2 weeks.
Example 2: **Late shipments**	
Late shipments noted on shipment log to be addressed by management.	Shipment log shows information such as volume trend, late deliveries and man-hours allocation. Over time hours showed an upward trend parallel with volume increase. There is a possible resource misallocation to match volume demand. Manager to further investigate; auditor will follow up in 2 weeks.

(Continued)

(Continued)

Table 2.1 Examples of auditing beyond compliance.

Conventional audit finding	Auditing beyond compliance (measurable metrics to evaluate success included)
Example 3: **Customer concern – verification of timely response**	
Response to customer complaints exceeds the internal requirement of 10 days. Department has to address this non-conformance to internal procedures.	Process flow for customer complaints processing was reviewed; records and interviews showed approximately 5 waiting days for customer service to gather all information, additional 10–25 days waiting time for process owners to complete investigation of root cause prior to submission to Quality Assurance for formal documentation. Additional information needed from process owners for submission to auditor: • Identify root causes of each hand-off delay (if any) • Identify realistic cut-off time for each hand-off
Example 4: **Preventive maintenance of equipment X**	
Records of required/planned preventive maintenance are completed. Program has flexibility for unplanned maintenance as needed. **No discrepancy noted.**	Records of required/planned preventive maintenance are complete. Program has flexibility for unplanned maintenance as needed; trend noted for unplanned fuse replacement higher than last period. (Although not a discrepancy, this was noted as symptom of system irregularity.) Process walk of the area discovered outer cover of equipment is not completely sealed, permitting water leakage inside the motor during water pressure cleaning of the area and causing fuse blow out. **Finding:** No trend monitoring or analysis of repeating incidents (such as replacement of blown fuse) to evaluate if action plan is needed.

(Continued)

(Continued)

Table 2.1 Examples of auditing beyond compliance.

Conventional audit finding	Auditing beyond compliance (measurable metrics to evaluate success included)
Example 5: **Seal integrity of sterilized pouch containing medical kits – random occurrence**	
Hospital complained that some sterilized pouches containing medical disposable kits are found with random scratches, tearing the sterilization barrier. This occurrence happens every other month. Manufacturer's auditors observed and reviewed all stages of the process and found no process variation that could have caused the random scratches at the manufacturing plant; it was therefore assumed that the random incident occurred at the point of use (such as hospital staff). Damaged kits were replaced and case was closed.	Recognition of the "vital few" clues is important in the audit of this example. The random defect has a pattern (such as occurrence of every other month). The defect indicates physical contact with the pouch. Based on these two parameters, the defect could be caused by common elements associated with the pouch (such as machine, manpower handling, storage area, and so on) that has possible monthly variation. Monitoring of these elements for 2 months revealed that the part-time operator working every other month has long fingernails that make scratch marks on the pouch during the packaging process. **Action item:** No workers with long nails allowed in the process; or operators must wear thick gloves to cover nails.

Understanding the methodology of auditing beyond compliance is the first step; aligning the goals or measurable metrics with the business plan is another challenge. The gears of the business plan and auditing beyond compliance initiatives must be synchronized to optimize full capability; otherwise, waste will be inevitable. Is the audit measuring significant metrics that will enhance compliance and add value? How does the audit function ensure alignment of the initiatives with the company plan?

AUDITING BEYOND COMPLIANCE—ALIGNMENT WITH THE BUSINESS PLAN

When aligning audit efforts with the business plan, audit management must first understand the many components of a business plan. In general, business components are geared to achieve growth and customer satisfaction (see Figure 2.1). These components have many interpretations and can be measured in various ways, depending on the company mission. The business plan is the guiding force that unites the core elements and key drivers of success unique to the company into one synchronized network. Treatment of these core elements as individual component will have a sub-optimization effect that will bring discord to the system's balance. The harmonious blending of these core elements will enhance system potential and make it possible to take advantage of synergy, strengthening the organization's chance for success. These phrases may seem abstract and it may be difficult to translate them into audit measurables properly aligned with the auditing beyond compliance philosophy. In plain words, alignment of the audit measurables should consider existing programs already in the system. Key drivers of success needed to integrate audit efforts include, but are not limited to, the following examples:

- Process Excellence
- Continuous Improvement
- Customer Satisfaction

These elements are commonly mentioned in company mission statements and business goals, but often are not totally understood by the workforce. Why?

Alignment with these business drivers is not a simple quest and this journey's final destination may not be perfectly aligned to the mapped target, something that must be considered. Just like a travel plan, basic variables must be defined before the start of this journey.

Unless the organization clearly defines the unique meaning of the key drivers applicable to its system, there will never be a solid collaborative effort to sustain an initiative. An auditing initiative that is totally irrelevant or isolated from the company mission will never successfully materialize. If it does, under this condition, it will have a painful and short life.

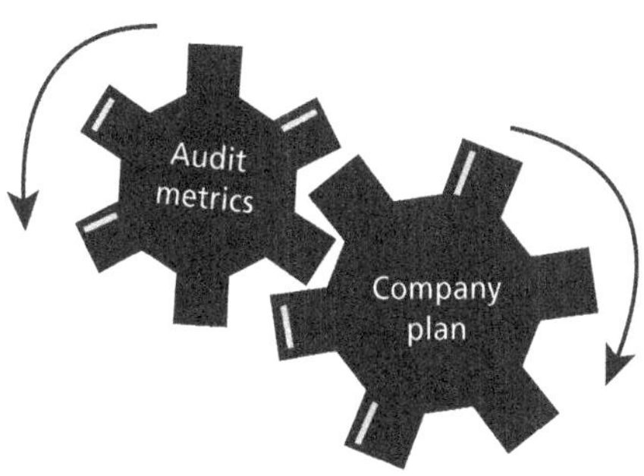

Figure 2.1 Audit metrics aligned with company plan.

How is the audit program aligned with the mission? This subject matter tends to be abstract or philosophical in nature and alignment is not always easy. One effective tool is open communication to clearly define the goals and expectations visibly supported by management and accepted at the grassroots level. The roadmap may have many turns and choices leading to countless combinations of results fueled by desired and realistic expectations. It is not an unrealistic goal to achieve this initiative if the roadmap is defined, understood, and supported within a closed-loop system that includes management and the entire workforce.

The interconnection of the typical elements in a business network is depicted in Figure 2.2.

Business key drivers and audit initiatives move as one unit.

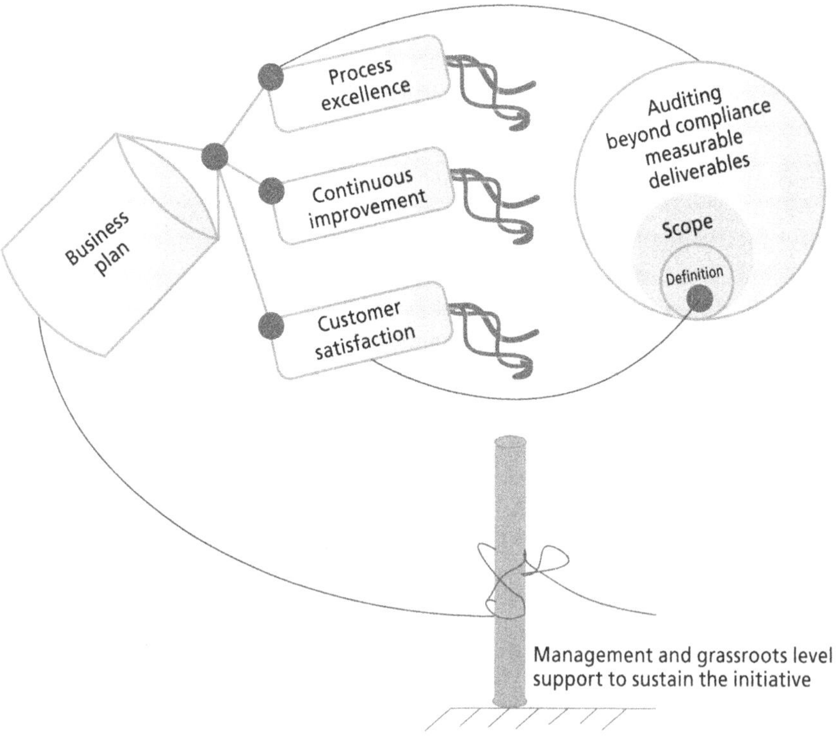

Figure 2.2 Alignment of the auditing beyond compliance model with the business plan.

3

Selection of Concept Transporter

Concept development by itself adds no value if not put into practice. Many tools are available for the realization of this concept, ranging from simple to highly complex strategies and techniques. For this publication, the selected "transporter" tool (such as the tool needed to carry out the deployment of strategies to convert concept into reality) is the Lean-Six Sigma (LSS) program. LSS is a time-tested system that has the flexibility and robustness to provide the roadmap for auditing beyond compliance.

The first stepping stone is promotion of the internal audit program's integration with LSS concepts into a cohesive and seamless alliance toward compliance and growth. This strategy may sound too complex, costly, and time consuming; for some, it is like embarking on a journey to an unknown territory. Not everyone is geared to undertake advanced statistical analysis or technical philosophies typically associated with LSS. This is a common fear about using LSS as an improvement tool, but it is not a true picture of the LSS concept! It is only complicated if the complicated tools are chosen.

LSS tools cover a wide spectrum of methods, ranging from basic to medium to highly complex, to serve diverse user applications and needs. LSS terminology may sound intimidating at first, but a few uses of the tools of your choice will widen your understanding and appreciation of what LSS can do for your company. The real challenge is the incorporation of these tools into a system that is pliable, simple, and yet sensitive enough to detect triggers and indicators of potential deviation as well as improvement opportunities.

Companies governed by multiple standards (for example, ISO 9001, AS9100, TL 9000, and FDA) are often reluctant to add LSS to the mix. The lack of understanding and exposure to this methodology leads most practitioners to believe that LSS is another roadblock and that it adds another tier of complication of the system. In fact, the integration of multiple quality standards under one system is simpler and more cost efficient than treating these quality standards individually as stand-alone requirements. The latter option, if chosen, will be expensive and a nightmare to audit! The solution to this dilemma is the creation of a model, an application engine (such as the LSS tools), and a documentation template integrating the multiple variables into a single system that functions just like a master key. This strategy is the focal point of this book.

How does one start the journey to this quest? Selling the concept to secure management support and buy-in is the ticket to a successful start. One need not be a LSS guru or Black Belt to undertake this challenge. It requires only motivation and a strong program to demonstrate the measurable benefits of using the LSS tool in auditing beyond compliance. Many programs can be utilized to achieve this goal, but this publication will focus on case models showing the application of LSS.

BUSINESS MISSION

"Go for the low-hanging fruit." This is a common saying in the business world, but is it logical? It depends on the benefits and risks involved. During the risk/benefit assessment, it is imperative that cost and improvement drivers are aligned with the business mission; otherwise, it will be a waste to allocate resources in this endeavor and deprive other areas. All opportunities are not of equal importance; their relevance and impact to the business mission dictate their priority level. Picking *any* low hanging fruit is not always practical; in some cases, this flawed priority practice can actually be a deterrent to improvement if initiatives are not aligned with the business plan. This break down in resource planning is synonymous with sub-optimization. In plain language, it is the misuse of valuable resources. Why is the understanding of this concept so important?

Auditing beyond compliance is a tool that should add value through the identification of improvement opportunities versus risks involved. Not all improvement initiatives count as added value if these are not aligned with the business mission. It is like perfecting the manufacturing of a swimwear design at optimized cost to target market share at the North Pole during the winter season.

Knowledge and understanding of the business mission are key in the development of a dynamic roadmap for auditing beyond compliance and effective program implementation using a concept transporter (such as Lean-Six Sigma tools) throughout the journey. Risk assessment is vital in this process.

Use the scale of scrutiny to evaluate project priority level (Figure 3.1). Initiatives are not all equal. Evaluate risks vs. benefits and choose initiatives based on alignment with business vision (not just *any* low-hanging fruit).

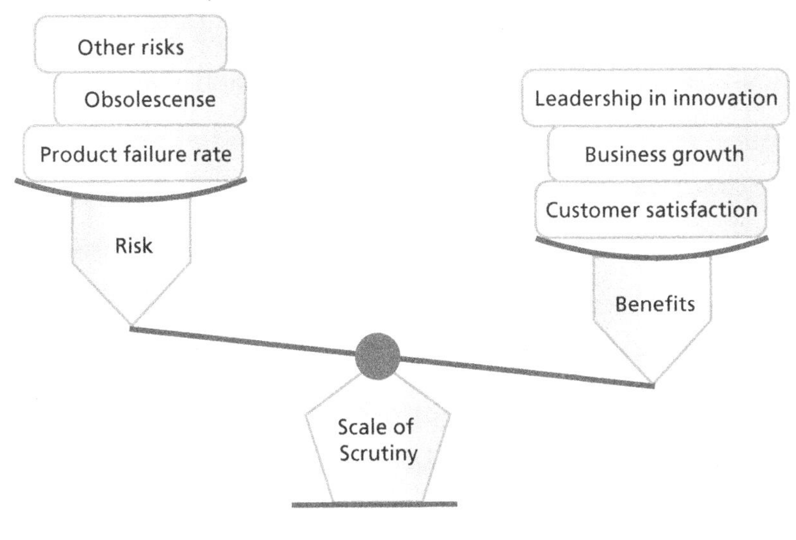

Figure 3.1 Scale of Scrutiny.

Does this mean skipping the audit of operations with lower impact to the business? No; doing that might jeopardize some contractual requirements on compliance verification and eliminate the opportunity to identify potential improvement and savings. Audits can be layered to cover a large scope over a short period of time to verify compliance and effectiveness at different phases of implementation. Audits done in layers or tiers are far more effective because the skill set and time frame for each layer or tier can vary according to the selected scope for each tier, making the audit system more flexible.

THE TIERED OR LAYERED AUDIT PROGRAM

A tiered or layered audit approach is useful as part of an escalation process in the deployment of the audit program (Figure 3.2):

- **Tier 1:** The focus of this activity is the verification of compliance against process work instructions and policies at the grassroots level. Recurring non-conformances at the deployment point may be assigned to this tier to increase accountability of compliance and to empower process owners who are typically the subject experts of day-to-day activities to discover sources of error and waste.
- **Tier 2:** The primary goal of this tier is to spot check Tier 1 audits performed by multifunctional teams to remove possible bias. This activity will also focus on improvement opportunities that may have been missed by the Tier 1 audit as the process owners performing Tier 1 may be too close to the process to see a broader vision.
- **Tier 3:** This is normally more expensive than Tier 1 and 2 audits and normally done less frequently due to the skill set requirement or complexity of the method involved. This is equivalent to the overall system audit performed by a designated company audit team. This is the top of the tiered audit hierarchy and should allow a better view of any gaps within the system.

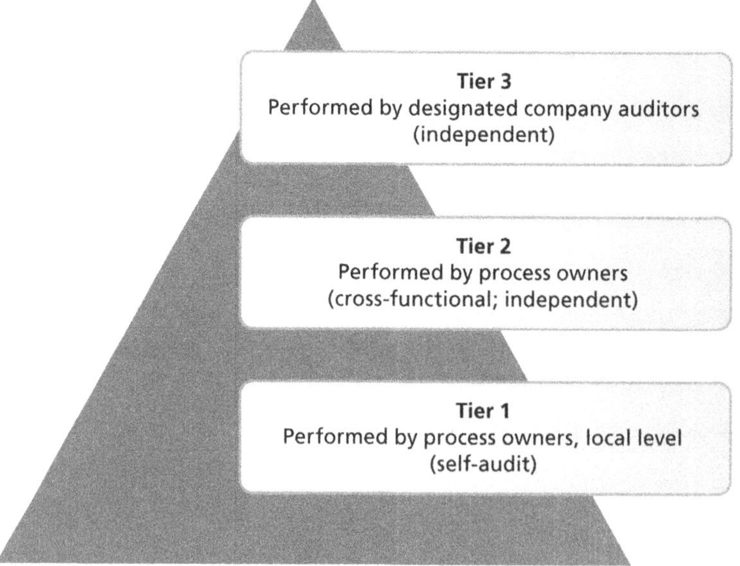

Figure 3.2 Tiered audit structure outline.

Tiered auditing can be a powerful strategy in casting a wider net of compliance monitoring and improvement initiatives in shorter cycles and optimizing the different skill sets of available resources. Timely feedback on system, process, or product performance at various phases of the operation will allow timely intervention and adjustment as needed. Tiers can be subdivided to optimize timing and coverage of the different audit categories—product, process, or systems—in an efficient fashion. The Tier 1 audit allows process owners periodic review of associated work instructions in order to verify or validate written instructions with actual practice or voice a best practice idea.

TRIBAL KNOWLEDGE

It is not rare to find that process owners have developed better, more efficient techniques that are within the bounds of written instructions. How is that possible? Process owners develop subject expertise through training, observation, and longevity in the service or through self-development. The process owner's absorption of learned information triggers the development of a personalized skill set that may result in customized execution of a task. This is known as "tribal knowledge." Is tribal knowledge good or bad? First of all, process owners must not deviate from written instructions, policies, or customer requirements without proper change approval. However, there are "gray areas" wherein application of tribal knowledge does not violate any of these requirements. Is this acceptable? In general, it is not acceptable to apply tribal knowledge without proper approval as it defeats the purpose of standardization for consistent output. Application of tribal knowledge is sometimes difficult to spot, but within the grassroots audits (Tiers 1 and 2 in Figure 3.2) there is increased chance of discovery. Tribal knowledge can be a source of improvement, as shown in this simple example:

> In addition to the "hot sheet" list required by the work instruction, one supervisor writes the daily job order priority sequence on a board displayed at the work area for easy viewing. The use of the board as visual standard is not required or mentioned on the work instruction, but it has been an effective guide in prioritizing the orders. The supervisor observed that it is more convenient to look at the daily board display instead of the hot sheet with many entries for the entire week. Is this a violation of the work instruction or an added value that should be made part of the work instruction? The auditor would be more concerned if this example of tribal knowledge, using the daily board display, were to become standard practice in lieu of the cumbersome weekly hot list.

Simple tribal knowledge such as this example may be missed during conventional audits, which are usually under time constraint and focused on critical compliance elements. Subtle events with significant impact such as the one described here may be easily missed. Tier 1 audits will normally spot these improvement opportunities because workers at the grassroots level are normally the creators of these techniques developed to aid them in their day-to-day tasks. The audit tier described in Figure 3.2 provides a platform for process owners or subject experts to voice out their contributions to process improvement and gain acknowledgment from peers and management. This empowerment tool serves as a motivational factor in robust workforce participation and deep involvement (that is, not superficial) in the program. The grassroots level audit is invaluable in keeping the workforce actively engaged in the different phases of the business; through grassroots level audits, the workforce benefits from "seeing" ongoing changes, opportunities for improvement, and other challenges that normally would not be visible for activities that are not part of their routine responsibilities. The grassroots level audits serve as another form of communication wherein information learned and shared can be utilized in various applications. The system can gain another side benefit from this activity—that is, notification of the workforce about documentation changes. Would it not be "killing two birds in one shot" if it were required that all document changes go through a grassroots level audit to verify effectiveness of the change? In this way, the process owners can critique and provide user feedback to identify a baseline reference point for future observations.

Figure 3.3 provides further details about the purpose and benefits of layered audits.

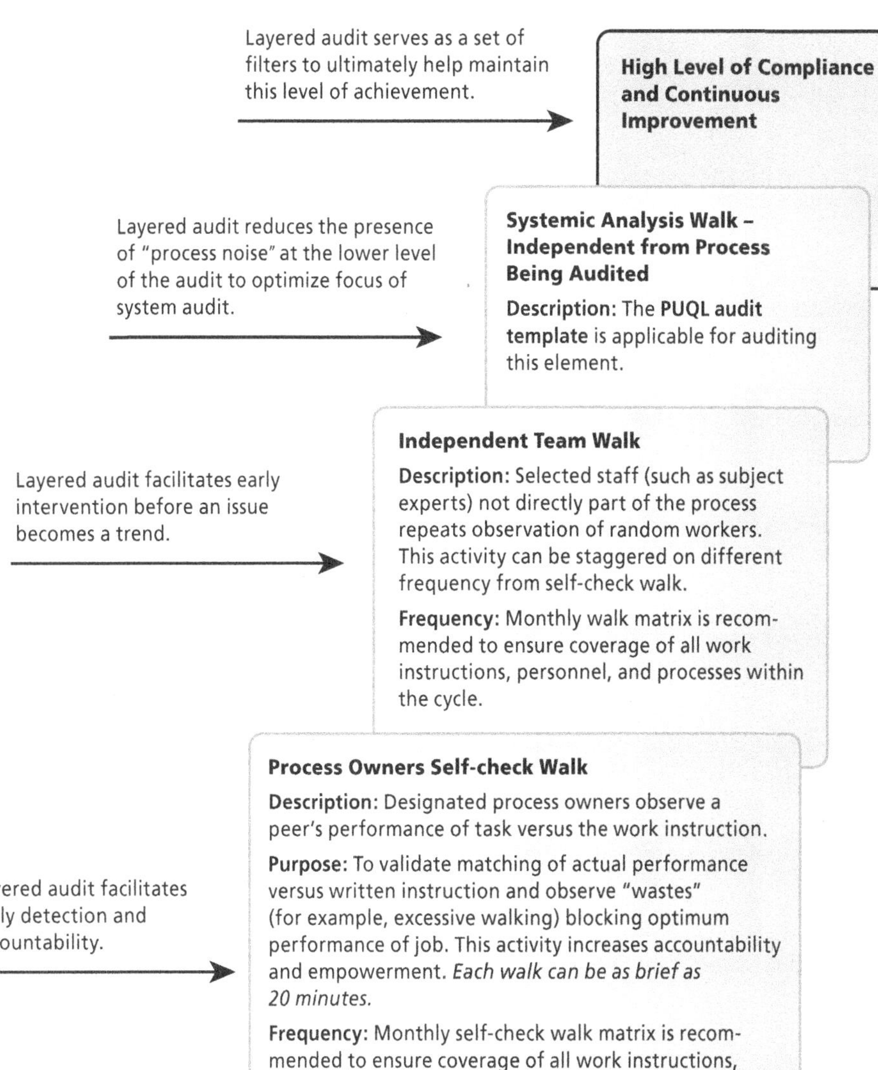

Layered audit serves as a set of filters to ultimately help maintain this level of achievement.
High Level of Compliance and Continuous Improvement
Layered audit reduces the presence of "process noise" at the lower level of the audit to optimize focus of system audit.
Systemic Analysis Walk – Independent from Process Being Audited
Description: The **PUQL audit template** is applicable for auditing this element.
Layered audit facilitates early intervention before an issue becomes a trend.
Independent Team Walk
Description: Selected staff (such as subject experts) not directly part of the process repeats observation of random workers. This activity can be staggered on different frequency from self-check walk.
Frequency: Monthly walk matrix is recommended to ensure coverage of all work instructions, personnel, and processes within the cycle.
Layered audit facilitates early detection and accountability.
Process Owners Self-check Walk
Description: Designated process owners observe a peer's performance of task versus the work instruction.
Purpose: To validate matching of actual performance versus written instruction and observe "wastes" (for example, excessive walking) blocking optimum performance of job. This activity increases accountability and empowerment. *Each walk can be as brief as 20 minutes.*
Frequency: Monthly self-check walk matrix is recommended to ensure coverage of all work instructions, personnel, and processes within the cycle.

Figure 3.3 Layered (tiered) audit: purpose and benefits.

4

Develop a Dynamic Universal Roadmap

The journey to auditing beyond compliance will have a higher probability of success if the roadmap design provides an optimal route with minimum inefficiencies and waste. Waste, if not identified and controlled, is likely to prevail in a setting with multiple quality standards (such as ISO 9001, industry regulations, customer-specific requirement, and so on) mandated by the customer base in a fast-paced environment where quick changeover is a must. This situation poses a challenge to maintain the required quality level regardless of circumstances through the constant verification of the quality program's effectiveness. Consistent and timely verification of these multiple standards can be a complex and expensive activity if the audit process is not streamlined to achieve a one-size-fits-all system design (or at least 80%–90% fit). How can this be achieved?

Streamlining the quality program to achieve a compliant, lean, and effective system is one path to a successful enterprise. This audit design is the focus of this publication.

It can be extremely cumbersome, expensive, and inefficient to create audit models for each individual quality standard and still maintain a timely cohesive program. One solution is to consolidate the different quality elements into a portable universal system driven by the application engine such as the Lean methodologies to a universal audit roadmap. Why portable and universal? This strategy is similar to the concept of a universal electrical power device. It bridges the gap between the different attributes of multiple systems plugged into the network. The converter aids in the seamless integration of these attributes to achieve a compatible connection within the system. Sounds complicated and abstract? On the contrary, it is quite simple. The key is the design of a Portable Universal Quality System (PUQL) model, integrated with LSS and documented in the PUQL template depicted in Figure 4.1.

Concept

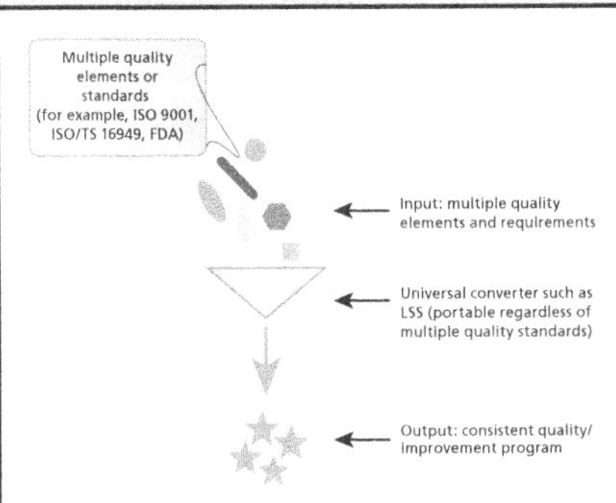

(This diagram is enlarged in Figure 4.2.)

The Portable Universal Quality Lean (PUQL)

This concept describes the integration of the different standards or requirements governing a system. Multiple standards will be cumbersome and expensive to audit individually using different techniques, audit methodologies, and checklists.

This is a visual explanation of the focus of this publication; integration of the multiple standards to simplify auditing beyond compliance.

A concept not implemented is static and only good as a paperweight.

Concept Transporter

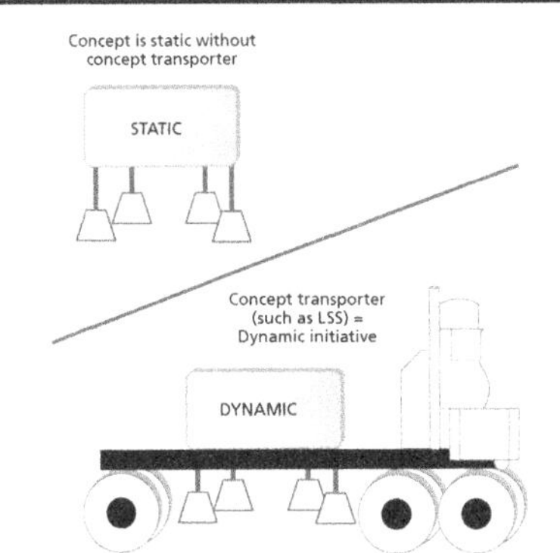

A concept transporter is a system or tool that facilitates application of the concept into practical use. The concept transporter chosen for this publication is Lean-Six Sigma (LSS) methodology.

Concept Converter

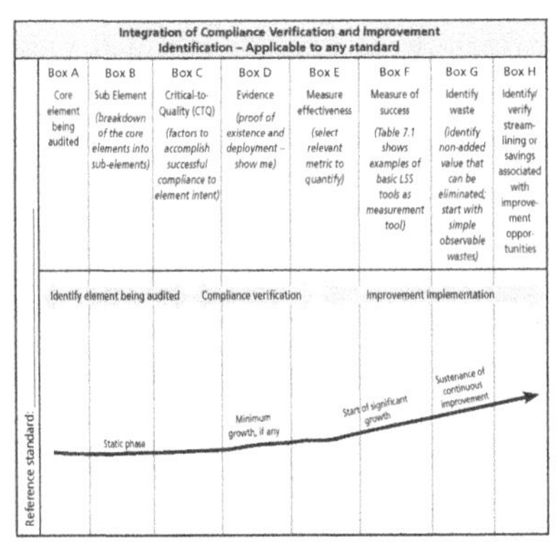

(This diagram is enlarged in Figure 4.3)

Audit findings are converted into measurable compliance, measurable success and improvement opportunities (and savings, as applicable) using a universal PUQL template.

This template has built-in detectors and signals for identification of compliance gaps and improvement opportunities.

This template not only simplifies the audit of multiple standards, but also provides guidelines in auditing beyond compliance.

Figure 4.1 PUQL phases: Concept ⟶ Concept Transporter ⟶ Concept Converter.

Auditing a system with more than one regulatory standard is a challenge that auditors can understand. Imagine auditing a system with multiple standards such as ISO 9001, ISO/TS 16949, AS9100, TL 9000, Mil-PRF standard, and FDA/Good Manufacturing Practices certifications, in addition to certain customer-specific requirements. Under resource and time constraints, the audit management of this pool of standards can be complicated and expensive. On top of these standards, the audit system must also address the different audit categories (product, process, and systems) to ensure coverage of all aspects of this program.

The Portable Universal Quality System model depicted in Figure 4.2 is a simple method that may be able to cover most, if not all, of these elements. This concept provides a simpler documentation of auditing beyond compliance—as well as an innovative template to incorporate identification of waste, improvement opportunities, and measurable deliverables.

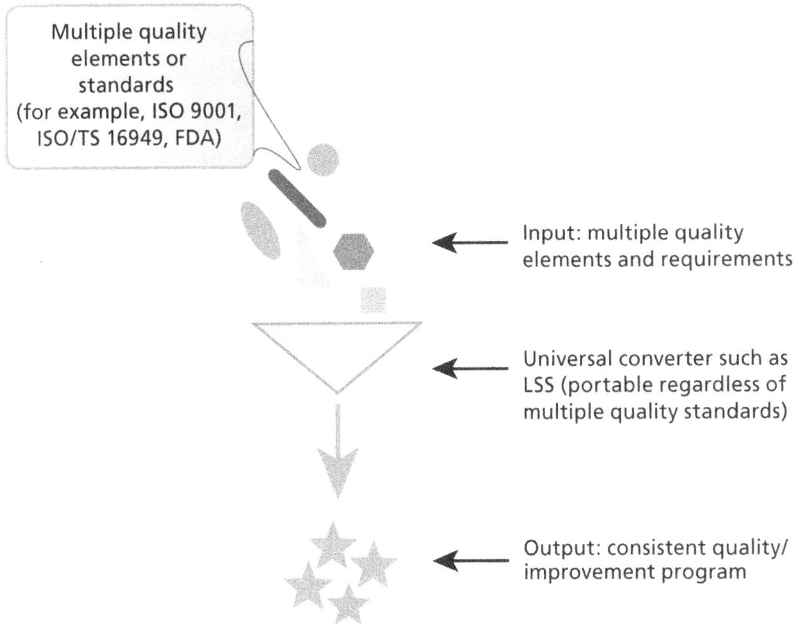

Figure 4.2 PUQL system concept.

Execution of the PUQL concept shown in Figure 4.2 seems abstract without an actual model or template as a guideline. Figure 4.3 illustrates the conversion of this concept into a template using the traditional elements of auditing (boxes A-D) supplemented by Lean-Six Sigma

(LSS) methods (boxes E-H). This simple template can be used to audit companies with one or multiple quality standards or regulatory requirements focusing on compliance and improvement. The growth line at the bottom shows that the compliance verification audit may trigger minimal growth or none, but the integration of LSS increases the probability of growth and improvement. This general roadmap will provide a repeatable process and a path to achieving an effective audit beyond compliance.

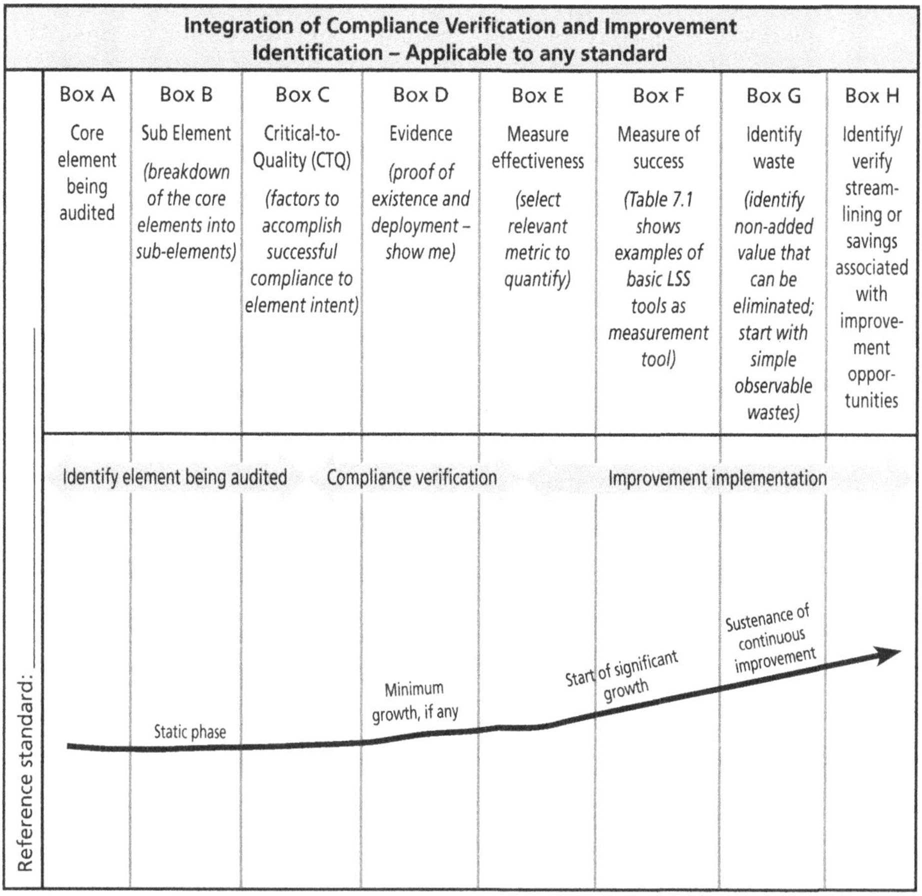

Integration of Compliance Verification and Improvement Identification – Applicable to any standard

Box A	Box B	Box C	Box D	Box E	Box F	Box G	Box H
Core element being audited	Sub Element *(breakdown of the core elements into sub-elements)*	Critical-to-Quality (CTQ) *(factors to accomplish successful compliance to element intent)*	Evidence *(proof of existence and deployment – show me)*	Measure effectiveness *(select relevant metric to quantify)*	Measure of success *(Table 7.1 shows examples of basic LSS tools as measurement tool)*	Identify waste *(identify non-added value that can be eliminated; start with simple observable wastes)*	Identify/verify stream-lining or savings associated with improvement opportunities

Identify element being audited — Compliance verification — Improvement implementation

Static phase — Minimum growth, if any — Start of significant growth — Sustenance of continuous improvement

Reference standard: ________

Figure 4.3 PUQL audit template.

This portable tool for integrating compliance and improvement is the focal point of this publication. This single template combines conventional auditing for compliance and the innovative integration of the application engine to generate the added value of improvement identification.

USING THE PUQL AUDIT TEMPLATE
(Figure 4.3)

1. **Choose the reference standard to be audited** and list it under the "Reference" box. The reference need not be a standard such as the ISO series; it can be a customer product requirement, process specification, or baseline for evaluation.

2. **Box A** – List the core element being audited. In the example in Figure 5.2, the core element under audit is "ISO 9001:2008, element 6.2- Human Resources."

3. **Box B** – List the sub-element (if any) or the breakdown of the core element under audit. In the example in Figure 5.2, the sub-element being audited is "sub-element 6.2.2"

   Note: If there is further breakdown of sub-elements, they can be listed under this column as applicable.

4. **Box C** – List the critical-to-quality (CTQ) metrics necessary to comply with the intent or the desired output of the element being audited. The strategic way to determine CTQ is to think of the element as a process or a machine that requires raw material (input) to produce a finished product (output).

5. **Box D** – List the relevant evidence to show compliance to this element. There are many options to show evidence. In example Figure 5.2, the chosen records audited to verify the competence of personnel performing work affecting conformity to product requirements are qualifications and training records.

6. **Box E** – Identify metrics to measure effectiveness of the chosen evidence noted on box D. The mere presence of the evidence listed in box D does not necessarily mean that the process is effective. There must be some measure of success or there is no benchmark of the performance status or a starting line for any future improvement. In selecting the metric, ensure that it is properly aligned with the desired output; measurement of the metric will provide indication of success.

7. **Box F** – List the Lean-Six Sigma tool used to analyze data; examples listed in Table 7.1. Basic LSS analysis tools provide another way for reviewing the information uncovered during the audit. These tools may be new to non-practitioners of LSS, but the tools are manageable and easy to understand, as explained in the following pages. Every scenario indicates an appropriate tool that can help the auditor reveal the subsurface interconnection of information based on the visible surface signals detected during the audit. Explanation of LSS tool features and actual application are shown in more detail in the next chapters.

8. **Box G** – List any observed wastes (no added value) that can be eliminated or streamlined to make the process more efficient. Some visible wastes observable during audits may be symptoms of roadblocks to improvement as well as hindrance to consistent compliance. Examples of wastes are:

   - Excessive transportation of resources
   - Excessive inventory
   - Excessive movement
   - Waiting time
   - Over-production
   - Over-processing
   - Defects
   - Sub-optimization of skills

   Detailed explanation and examples of wastes can be found in the following pages.

9. **Box H** – List improvement opportunities identified in box G for follow up on the verification audit. The improvement opportunities may be as simple as reducing wastes to streamline the process.

5

Application of the PUQL Audit Model – A Flexible Tool

This chapter illustrates actual application of the PUQL model discussed in Chapter 4 and shows critical-to-quality (CTQ) and measurable metrics typical for quality elements. The input variables listed in the PUQL template are examples only. These variables will be different for each situation dependent on the company-specific business format and operational data.

The PUQL audit model not only simplifies the integration of the compliance and improvement partnership during the audit of any standard. It is applicable regardless of the audit type (quality systems, product, or process). The auditor has flexibility and full control of the core and sub-elements to be audited, as well as the extent of the audit scope. A single or multiple PUQL audit template may be used to document the chosen breakdown of elements and sub-elements. Audits using the PUQL model may be done by one or multiple auditors, depending on the element breakdown, and still maintain consistency of the audit methodology and reporting.

The PUQL model also allows multi-functional auditors to divide the audit of each PUQL variable, optimizing their areas of expertise (for example, the compliance portion to be verified by a quality team and the improvement portion by another team such as LSS or engineering). This is just one option. Think outside the box—there are many more.

The PUQL audit template is an effective compliance and improvement tool. The following pages show examples of PUQL use in the audit of various elements and customer requirements. Information needed to complete the template is user dependent; actual use will vary depending on evidence, sampling, and other details available during the audit.

Portable Lean Audit Template Integration of compliance verification and improvement identification – applicable to any standard								
Reference standard: ISO 9001:2008 – 4.2.4 Control of Records	Box A	Box B	Box C	Box D	Box E	Box F	Box G	Box H
	Core element *(breakdown of core elements into sub-elements)*	**Sub-element** *(breakdown of core elements into sub-elements)*	**Critical-to-Quality (CTQ)** *(examples of factors to meet intent of element being audited)*	**Evidence** *(proof of existence and/or deployment – show me)*	**Measure effectiveness** *(select metric to quantify effectiveness)*	**Measure of success** *(Table 7.1 shows details on the use of the LSS measurement tools)*	**Identify waste** *(identify non-added value that can be eliminated; start with simple observable waste)*	**Identify or verify savings** (savings *associated with improvement opportunities)*
	Element being audited		Compliance verification			Improvement implementation		
	4.2.4 Control of Records	*"The organization shall establish a documented procedure to define the controls needed for the identification, storage, protection, retrieval, retention and disposition of records."*	CTQs to include but not limited to: a. **Documented procedure** containing provisions for all the elements mentioned in column B.	a. **Sampling of quality records** Check archive system to verify storage protection, easy retrieval, and so on.	a. **Completeness and accuracy of Master Device Records** or complete service/product paperwork against required traceability records. *(for example, using forward or backward traceability verification, such as verification of documents from raw materials to finished product or vice versa)*	a. **Process flow of** information or documents showing the number of records handling or 'touches' (For example, is the material specification sheet available upon receipt of product or Receiving inspector opens incoming boxes looking for the paper?)	a. **Examples of waste:** Wasted time spent looking for paperwork. (Can paperwork be in electronic form for easier handling and retrieval?)	a. **Savings** (audit cost before and after implementation of savings from waste reduction uncovered in Box G.)

Figure 5.1 PUQL audit of documentation requirements.

Portable Lean Audit Template Integration of compliance verification and improvement identification – applicable to any standard								
Reference standard: ISO 9001:2008 – 6.2 Human Resources	Box A	Box B	Box C	Box D	Box E	Box F	Box G	Box H
	Core element *(breakdown of core elements into sub-elements)*	**Sub-element** *(breakdown of core elements into sub-elements)*	**Critical-to-Quality (CTQ)** *(examples of factors to meet intent of element being audited)*	**Evidence** *(proof of existence and/or deployment – show me)*	**Measure effectiveness** *(select metric to quantify effectiveness)*	**Measure of success** *(Table 7.1 shows details on the use of the LSS measurement tools)*	**Identify waste** *(identify non-added value that can be eliminated; start with simple observable waste)*	**Identify or verify savings** *(savings associated with improvement opportunities)*
	Element being audited		Compliance verification			Improvement implementation		
	6.2 Human Resources	6.2.2 *"(a) the organization shall determine the necessary competence for personnel performing work affecting conformity to product requirement"*	CTQs to include but not limited to: a. **Accurate job descriptions** showing requirements for each personnel job category. b. **Clear Instructions or standards used** by personnel to show requirements of jobs being performed. c. **Clear acceptance criteria** required for the process/system or product being audited.	a. **Qualifications or training records** of personnel vs. job descriptions b. **Sampling of personnel** for observation or interview vs. required task on the work instructions to asses knowledge of requirements. c. **Sampling of process or product output** vs. acceptance criteria	a. **Rejection or error rate** or complaint trend associated with task being audited b. **on-time completion**	a. **Trend analysis (Pareto analysis)** of error rate This will help identify the vital few recurring errors associated with the process under audit. Root cause analysis of the defect occurrence will help pinpoint primary reason for the occurrence. This will also identify or eliminate training issue as the cause.	a. **Examples of waste:** Reduction of error rate costs (wasted resource time, material) associated with this process before and after uncovering and resolving root causes discovered in column F.	a. **Savings** (audit cost before and after implementation of savings from waste reduction uncovered in Box G.)

Figure 5.2 PUQL audit of human resources.

Portable Lean Audit Template
Integration of compliance verification and improvement identification – applicable to any standard

Reference standard: ISO 9001:2008 – 8.3 Control of Non-Conforming Product

Box A	Box B	Box C	Box D	Box E	Box F	Box G	Box H
Core element *(breakdown of core elements into sub-elements)*	**Sub-element** *(breakdown of core elements into sub-elements)*	**Critical-to-Quality (CTQ)** *(examples of factors to meet intent of element being audited)*	**Evidence** *(proof of existence and/or deployment – show me)*	**Measure effectiveness** *(select metric to quantify effectiveness)*	**Measure of success** *(Table 7.1 shows details on the use of the LSS measurement tools)*	**Identify waste** *(identify non-added value that can be eliminated; start with simple observable waste)*	**Identify or verify savings** (savings associated with improvement opportunities)
Element being audited		Compliance verification			Improvement implementation		
8.3 Control of Non-Conforming Product "Organization shall ensure that product which does not conform to product requirements is identified and controlled to prevent its unintended use or delivery...."	*"Where applicable, the organization shall deal with non-conforming product by...* *a. taking action to eliminate the detected non-conformity"*	CTQs to include but not limited to: a. **Documented work instruction** defining controls and responsibilities dealing with non-conformities. b. **Proper segregation or identification** of non-conforming materials c. **Proper disposition** of the detected non-conformity	a. **Sampling of a** non-conforming material processing versus documented instruction b. **Sampling of the quarantine** area (OSD – overage, shortage and damage materials segregation area).	a. Number **of complaints** relating to material mix-up. b. **Record of non-conforming materials** versus physical verification (as applicable).	a. **Process flow** to identify error-proofing movement, containment and resolution of non-conforming material.	a. **Examples of waste:** Excess movement or waiting time associated in containing non-conforming materials.	a. **Savings** (audit cost before and after implementation of savings from waste reduction uncovered in Box G.)

Figure 5.3 PUQL audit of control of non-conforming material.

Portable Lean Audit Template
Integration of compliance verification and improvement identification – applicable to any standard

Reference standard: ISO 9001:2008 – 8.2.2 Internal Audit

Box A	Box B	Box C	Box D	Box E	Box F	Box G	Box H
Core element *(breakdown of core elements into sub-elements)*	**Sub-element** *(breakdown of core elements into sub-elements)*	**Critical-to-Quality (CTQ)** *(examples of factors to meet intent of element being audited)*	**Evidence** *(proof of existence and/or deployment – show me)*	**Measure effectiveness** *(select metric to quantify effectiveness)*	**Measure of success** *(Table 7.1 shows details on the use of the LSS measurement tools)*	**Identify waste** *(identify non-added value that can be eliminated; start with simple observable waste)*	**Identify or verify savings** (savings associated with improvement opportunities)
Element being audited		Compliance verification			Improvement implementation		
8.2.2 Internal Audit	*"(b) Effectively implemented and maintained…"*	CTQs to include but not limited to: a. **Planned intervals** (for example, schedule) b. **Audit program** to contain provisions for following elements: audit criteria, scope, frequency, methods, auditor selection, prioritization of process, review of previous audit results, recording requirements, verification/closure.	a. **Audit schedule** versus list of elements required by the standard being audited. B. **Audit procedure** provision for audit elements	a. **Completion rate** (listing on schedule match completed reports) b. **Trend analysis** (positive trend=success) (Clustering of similar individual findings may provide more visibility of a trend instead of reporting the discrepancies as individual occurrences).	a. **SIPOC** (Supplier-Input-Output-Customer) b. **VSM (value stream map)** to ensure all core processes are included in the audit plan.	a. **Efficiency/** optimization of the audit program such as cost or manpower allocation for the audit. For example, can certain elements be combined to reduce travel/etc?	a. **Savings** (Audit cost before and after implementation of savings from waste reduction uncovered in Box G.)

Figure 5.4 PUQL audit of internal audit.

Portable Lean Audit Template Integration of compliance verification and improvement identification – applicable to any standard								
	Box A	Box B	Box C	Box D	Box E	Box F	Box G	Box H
	Core element *(breakdown of core elements into sub-elements)*	**Sub-element** *(breakdown of core elements into sub-elements)*	**Critical-to-Quality (CTQ)** *(examples of factors to meet intent of element being audited)*	**Evidence** *(proof of existence and/or deployment – show me)*	**Measure effectiveness** *(select metric to quantify effectiveness)*	**Measure of success** *(Table 7.1 shows details on the use of the LSS measurement tools)*	**Identify waste** *(identify non-added value that can be eliminated; start with simple observable waste)*	**Identify or verify savings** *(savings associated with improvement opportunities)*
	Element being audited		Compliance verification			Improvement implementation		
Reference standard: C-TPAT: 4.3 Container Seals	4.3 Container Seals Written procedures must stipulate how seals are to be controlled and affixed to loaded containers.	*"Procedures must be in place for recognizing and reporting compromised seals and containers to US Border Protection...."*	CTQs to include but not limited to: a. **Seal control procedure** to address requirements noted in Box A of this template. b. **Seal inventory log accuracy** c. **Verifiable traceability tracking**	a. Evidence of seal procedure deployment and training of process owners. b. Accuracy of inventory: Physical seal inventory versus seal history log. c. Sample container traceability history and match listed seal number against seal inventory log.	a. Evidence of workforce understanding of the regulation (for example, interview or observation against procedure). b. Accuracy must be 100%, or a justifiable explanation must be included if there is discrepancy (for example, seal voided as trailer was re-opened to add more freight, seal replaced).	a. **SIPOC** (Supplier-Input-Output-Customer)	a. **Efficiency:** Is the storage of seals accessible at the point of use; is there excessive walking, waiting? Is the recording of the log convenient and not time consuming? (is the Bill of Lading accessible to immediately note the seal number or does the process require walking/ re-writing to transfer information?)	a. **Savings** in time/ movement (before and after) if information in Box G is improved.

Figure 5.5 PUQL audit of container seals (Custom Trade Partnership Against Terrorism Security policy).

Reference standard: 100–1 Customer Requirement – Batch order for 400 donuts is always short by about 25% for the last 2 weeks.

Portable Lean Audit Template Integration of compliance verification and improvement identification – applicable to any standard							
Box A	Box B	Box C	Box D	Box E	Box F	Box G	Box H
Core element *(breakdown of core elements into sub-elements)*	**Sub-element** *(breakdown of core elements into sub-elements)*	**Critical-to-Quality (CTQ)** *(examples of factors to meet intent of element being audited)*	**Evidence** *(proof of existence and/or deployment – show me)*	**Measure effectiveness** *(select metric to quantify effectiveness)*	**Measure of success** *(Table 7.1 shows details on the use of the LSS measurement tools)*	**Identify waste** *(identify non-added value that can be eliminated; start with simple observable waste)*	**Identify or verify savings** (savings associated with improvement opportunities)
Element being audited		Compliance verification			Improvement implementation		
100–1 Written procedures require processing of one batch of donuts (400 units) per order for Customer A.	Observed flow versus procedures matched: Formed donuts come out of 4 conveyor lines (100 units for each Conveyor | Oven | Quick freeze | Conveyor visual spot checking for any obvious non-conformance such as deformed, color | Automatic boxing | Automatic weighing/ labeling | Shipping	CTQs to include but not limited to: a. Outcoming 400 donuts coming from 4 conveyors from Quick freeze must be within the visual spot check standard	a. Evidence – Batch quality records – Weight historical records – Oven and Quick freeze settings versus specifications – Calibration records versus specifications **Findings:** Calibration of scale X was out of specification causing miscalculation of raw materials and shortage by approx 25%; only detected during weighing at packaging (too late). Workers compensate by replenishing shortage from next batch, etc. instead of reporting issue.	a. Action taken by process manager: Line clearance and start-up checklist to be performed before shift run (and should include equipment check). This checklist can be the metric for the process. Non-conformances noted can be trended to measure process/ resource performance.	a. The checklist stated in Box E can be the monitoring tool of process owners and can be easily verified during audits. b. Trend charts can also be used to monitor the parameters as baseline for improvement.	a. Identify waste such as rejection rate (cost of material/ labor) due to errors.	a. **Savings** in time/ movement (before and after) if information in Box G is improved.

Figure 5.6 PUQL audit of customer requirement: order completion process.

6

Lean-Six Sigma (LSS) Tools Integrated with the Audit Program

OPEN COMMUNICATION, NOT SILOS

Team effort requires realistic expectations and open communication (no silos). Understanding expectations behind the initiative provides a clearer insight for defining deliverables as measurements of success. Failure to break down the expectations of an audit event is a common occurrence, not necessarily due to the technical complexity normally associated with this initiative. It's due to a very simple factor: lack of communication. The gap between the vision, strategy, and tactical deployment loop can be easily bridged with the removal of silos that act as barriers obstructing the fluidity of knowledge exchange within the system. The accomplishment of realistic deliverables depends heavily on the free flow of information to and from the stakeholders (internal and external loops) as opposed to the "trickling" effect of selected data disseminated typical of a silo. Shown in Figure 6.1 are the two major types of information flow.

Once these two types of communication flow are identified and acknowledged, it will be easier to augment existing communication efforts until the structure is fortified for long-term implementation.

Communication issues are not easily detected during an audit, and may result in missed opportunities for improvement. It may be necessary to perform root cause analysis to determine the source of failure to achieve process excellence. The following scenario is an example of communication failure.

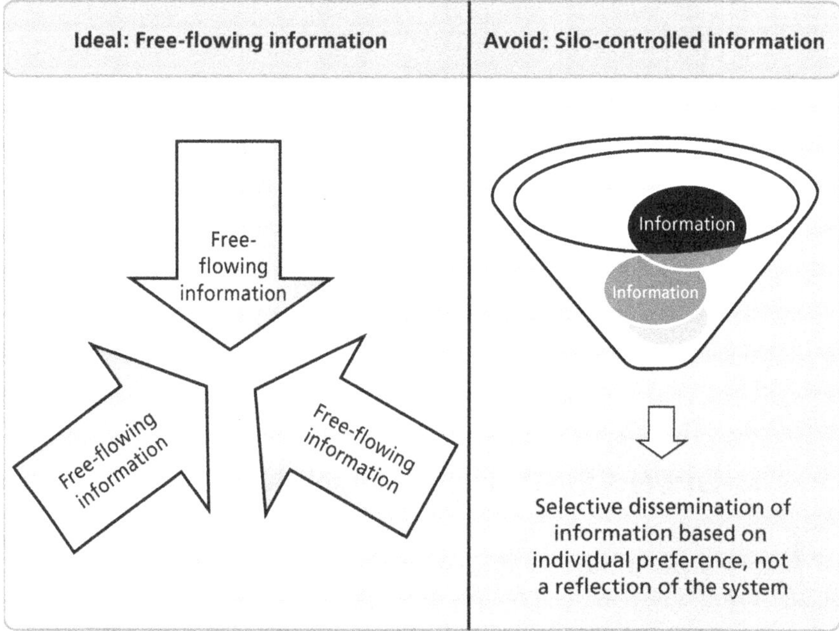

Figure 6.1 Major types of information flow.

Scenario: A team composed of Lean engineers and other staff was tasked to coordinate the Lean projects. This cross-functional team was selected to ensure alignment of the projects with the company mission and newly updated business plan. During the course of project selection, one of the senior engineers decided to limit the communication loop until the mid-phase of the project. This was done to maintain full control of the project scope and direction in order to prioritize certain areas of interest to the team (a silo). At the end of the project the results, as expected, benefited one area but failed to cast a wider net to cover higher risk areas (resulting in sub-optimization).

Result: Management expectation was not met.

Lesson Learned: Project selection was modified to include approval from the designated management team. Project selection and milestones were published to a wider audience for more visibility. The free-flowing mode of information will be the applicable tool for this event.

SIPOC

A Supplier-Input-Process-Output-Customer (SIPOC) diagram is a problem solving or analysis tool that reveals the breakdown of elements associated with the issue under evaluation. The method described in this section is just one of many techniques for the application of the SIPOC diagram.

Before the SIPOC diagram can be used, a key question must be answered: What is the problem and what is the reason for this analysis? Analysis of any process or system is normally triggered if the desired result is at risk or there are unknown variables affecting the performance level. These are just a few examples of triggers for a SIPOC application: there are many more. SIPOC is a flexible analysis tool that may be used in problem solving following a failure or as an early detection tool to identify possible roadblocks and failure modes. Depending on the situation that triggers its use, the SIPOC journey begins by answering a key question: What is the problem and what is the reason for this analysis?

Once these questions are answered, the SIPOC journey can begin. Knowing the problem or issue at hand will be the first milestone reached in identifying the connecting elements and process or system associated directly or indirectly with the issue under evaluation.

Every process, regardless of simplicity or complexity, has input and output elements impacting desired expectations or performance level. The selection of these elements is key in identifying the core drivers needed to meet the goal.

However, choosing the critical elements can sometimes be overwhelming, especially if there are numerous variables available for selection. Which ones are the vital few? The selection of these core variables is dependent on many factors, typically based on the risk assessment. The SIPOC diagram helps focus attention on the desired output and "weed out" other variables with little or no impact on the outcome.

One approach to effectively use the SIPOC diagram is "thinking backward," defining the desired output first to focus on the input most likely to achieve this outcome. Confusing? Here is a simple analogy:

> Baking cookies is a process (mixing ingredients, shaping cookies, baking at required temperature) that requires ingredients (input). The ingredients will differ for each type of cookies (output). Thinking backward, one should first define the desired output (chocolate chip cookies or sugar cookies?). Defining the output will dictate the type of ingredients needed to complete the process (input). The supplier of the ingredients will be the grocery store

and the customer is the person who requested the cookies. In summary, the SIPOC for baking cookies looks like this:

S – Supplier of ingredients: grocery store

I – Input: ingredients

P – Process: baking (combine ingredients, pre-heat oven at desired temperature, form dough, put on cookie sheet, bake at required time cycle)

O – Output: cookies

C – Customer: requestor of cookies

This is SIPOC in the simplest form!

Figure 6.2 is a SIPOC diagram for a corrective action program. The trigger for this SIPOC sample analysis is the need to define a compliant and effective corrective action program to prevent failure.

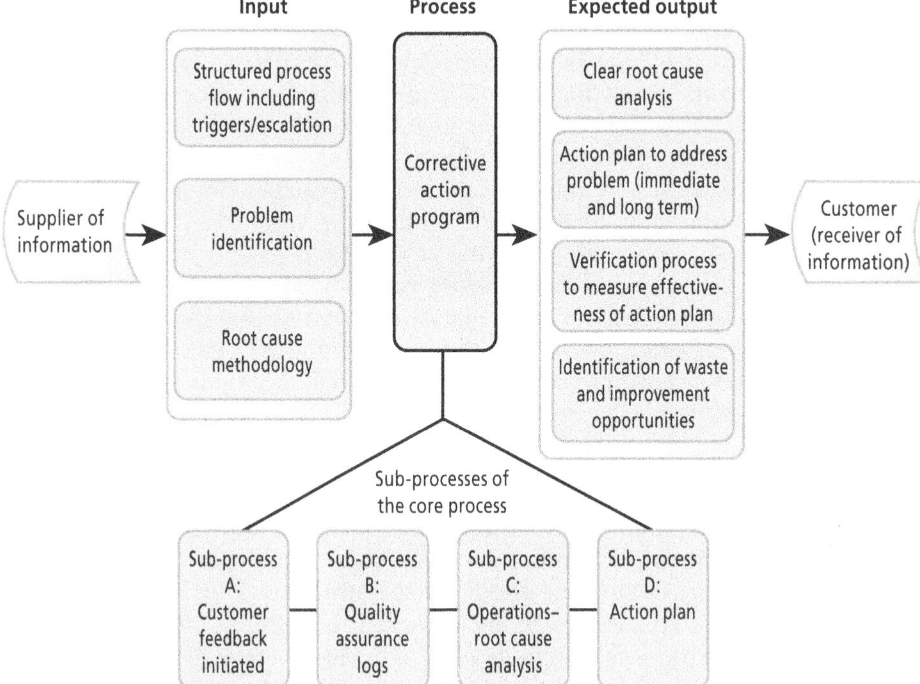

Figure 6.2 Typical SIPOC diagram for a corrective action program.

Thinking backward, it's possible to list the desired output from a corrective action program at the start of the diagram process. What are the expectations from a compliant and effective corrective action program? Once these core output elements are identified, it will be easier to uncover the relevant input critical to quality. What elements will impact the realization of the desired output aligned with the customer requirements?

Of course it's possible to design a program outlining the milestones needed to reach the desired output without using a SIPOC diagram. SIPOC is a tool that helps visualize this path in a methodical way and helps document the evaluation blueprint.

In itemizing the elements of the SIPOC diagram, it is important to note that in some cases multiple inputs will be available. Do not let the selection process be a roadblock; choose the primary inputs (the vital few) that will likely have major impact on the desired output. How do you select the vital few? Selection may be based on many factors including risk assessment, customer requirement, and financial impact. A SIPOC diagram of the same process will change depending on the variables, which are as dynamic as the business plan and company mission. The priority level of one element may drastically shift along with changes within the company environment or outside forces such as market trends. It is therefore imperative to have appropriate triggers in place to continue the gap analysis of the system. Business is a dynamic entity. A program that is stable and compliant today may drastically change tomorrow. Subtle changes, such as a staggered customer service work schedule to cover the night shift, may impact the customer concern escalation process listed as a critical input element in the SIPOC diagram. In this example, changes in the schedule reduced the day hours available to handle the majority of incoming customer telephone calls and caused an increase in customer complaints. This situation could have been resolved or mitigated with simple real-time communication with customer. Risk assessment needs further study to determine the impact and/or resolution of this new situation resulting from a subtle change.

The lesson learned in this example is that processes and systems are continually changing over time. Even the pyramids and mighty mountains change with continuing exposure to weather, erosion, and other environmental impacts; luckily, most process and systems changes can be contained and controlled to an acceptable level. Tools such as SIPOC are important aids in this process.

Sub-processes may be further analyzed to uncover hidden information buried in SIPOC diagram process layers. To describe this "SIPOC within a SIPOC" technique, a coined expression "S-Square" will be used in this publication. It may be time consuming to break down sub-processes using the S-Square technique; discretion should be used in deciding whether this effort will yield further information that will contribute to the desired output. Figure 6.3 illustrates S-Square technique, further breaking down sub-process D originally analyzed in the original SIPOC format (Figure 6.2).

A simplified SIPOC diagram is illustrated in Figure 6.4.

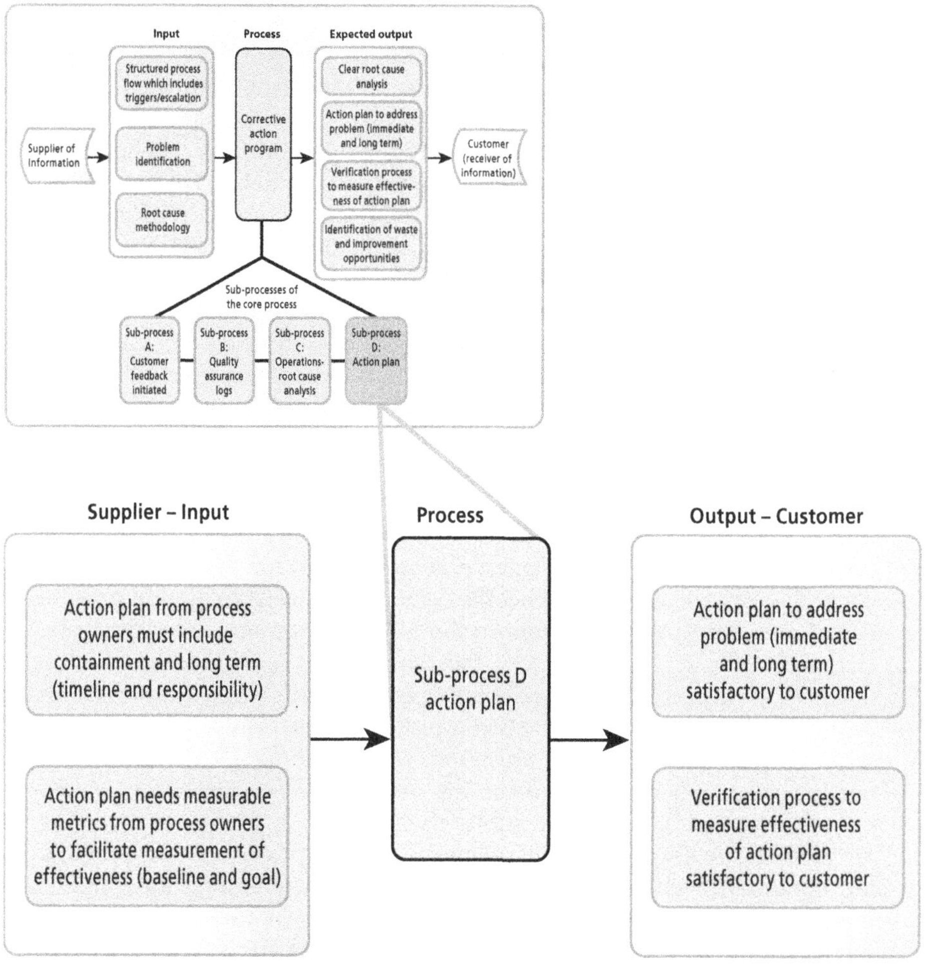

Input for the *Action Plan* process shows critical-to-quality metrics needed to achieve the overall output expected. The components of the Action Plan impact at least two of the expect outputs.

Figure 6.3 S-Square layout of sub-process D.

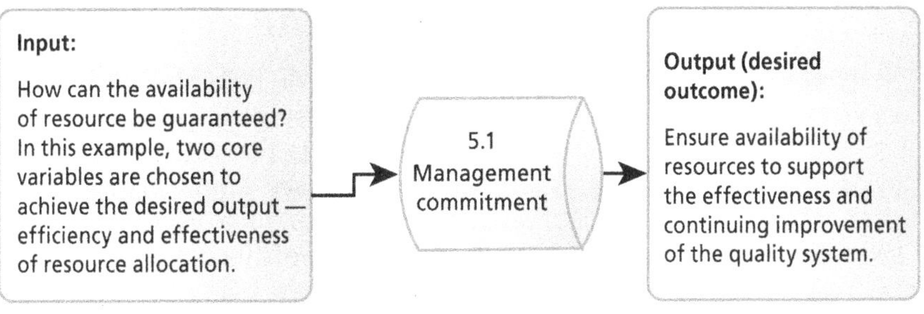

Figure 6.4 Simplified SIPOC diagram.

Figure 6.5 illustrates the use of a simple flowchart to analyze the effectiveness of process variables and measurements. The measure of effectiveness in this example is the comparison of the cycle time required by the customer with actual process capability using the resource allocated for the process. In this example, the cycle time (10 hours) is longer than the customer's expectation (8 hours); therefore, customer expectation cannot be met without a change on the status quo. Current process does not meet the intent of the element.

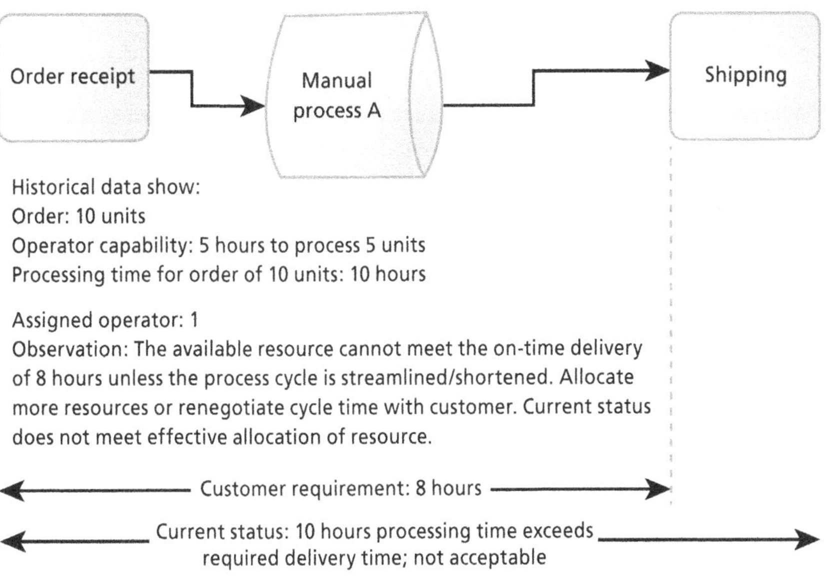

Figure 6.5 Analysis of evidence using a simple flowchart and cycle time review.

VALUE STREAM MAP

Understanding the basic process cycle will help the audit focus on areas that are either not compliant or in need of improvement. One LSS tool that will be useful for this purpose is the value stream map (VSM). This tool can be a simple flowchart (see Figure 6.6) showing cycle parameters such as time and roadblocks such as waiting time. The following case study shows a simple use of the VSM as an audit analysis tool.

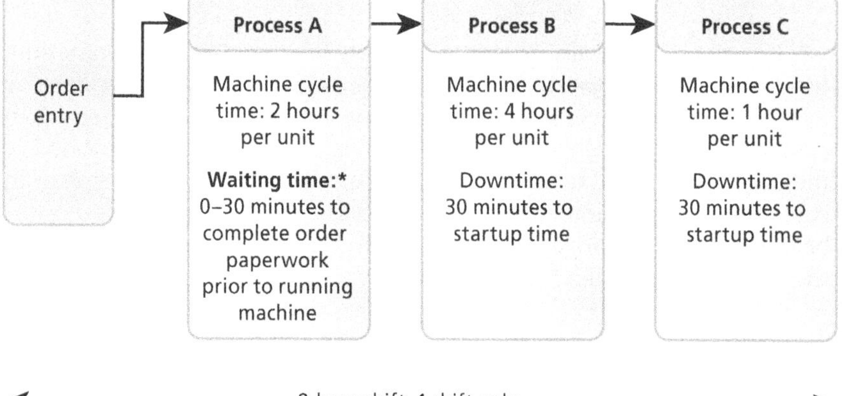

*Waiting time for process A to receive material certificates prior to starting process A machine ranges from 0–30 minutes. Waiting time is zero if paperwork is present upon material arrival at the plant.

The waiting time may be addressed in many ways (for example, request advance hard copy or electronic copy of the material paperwork for each shipment). It may be a good idea to evaluate downtime for process B and C to identify opportunities for streamlining.

Figure 6.6 Value stream map of product X.

Scenario: Timeliness of the completion of product X is not reliable, as shown in Figure 6.6. In some cases, a unit can be completed in an eight-hour shift; in some cases overtime is incurred to complete the product. The machine cycles and normal start-up downtime are fixed and should be adequate to complete the product in an eight-hour shift.

Analysis of Results Using VSM: The total of the three constant cycles and downtime (processes A, B, and C – shown in Figure 6.6) are sufficient to complete the order of one unit. Fluctuation in completion rate is caused by the waiting time variable during order entry (0–30 minutes). If paperwork is complete at order entry point, there is no waiting time; machines can be started on time to complete the order within the eight-hour shift without overtime. This roadblock can probably be uncovered without the use of VSM; however, the VSM increases the visibility of roadblocks such as the paperwork delay during order entry. With the problem (such as waiting time / waste) identified, focus can be tuned to the improvement action to address this element.

FISHBONE DIAGRAM

The fishbone diagram, just like any other analysis tool, is only effective if the input is accurate. What is the main input? It's important to understand the situation under evaluation and identify the problem as a starting point in using the fishbone methodology. In Figure 6.7, the problem represents the fish head attached to the individual bones or core variables relating to the problem. This interconnectivity provides a path in the detection of the primary elements with significant impact on the problem.

The fishbone diagram facilitates uncovering the core variables that have both direct and indirect impact on the problem. Once these variables are identified, the problem analysis can then focus on the vital few variables to drill down on the hidden root cause(s).

Typical variables considered in this methodology include, but are not limited to, the 6Ms: **M**aterial, **M**anpower, **M**other Nature (environment), **M**achine, **M**ethod, and **M**easurement. In some cases, it may be applicable to list the key processes and roadblocks associated with the problem (instead of the 6Ms).

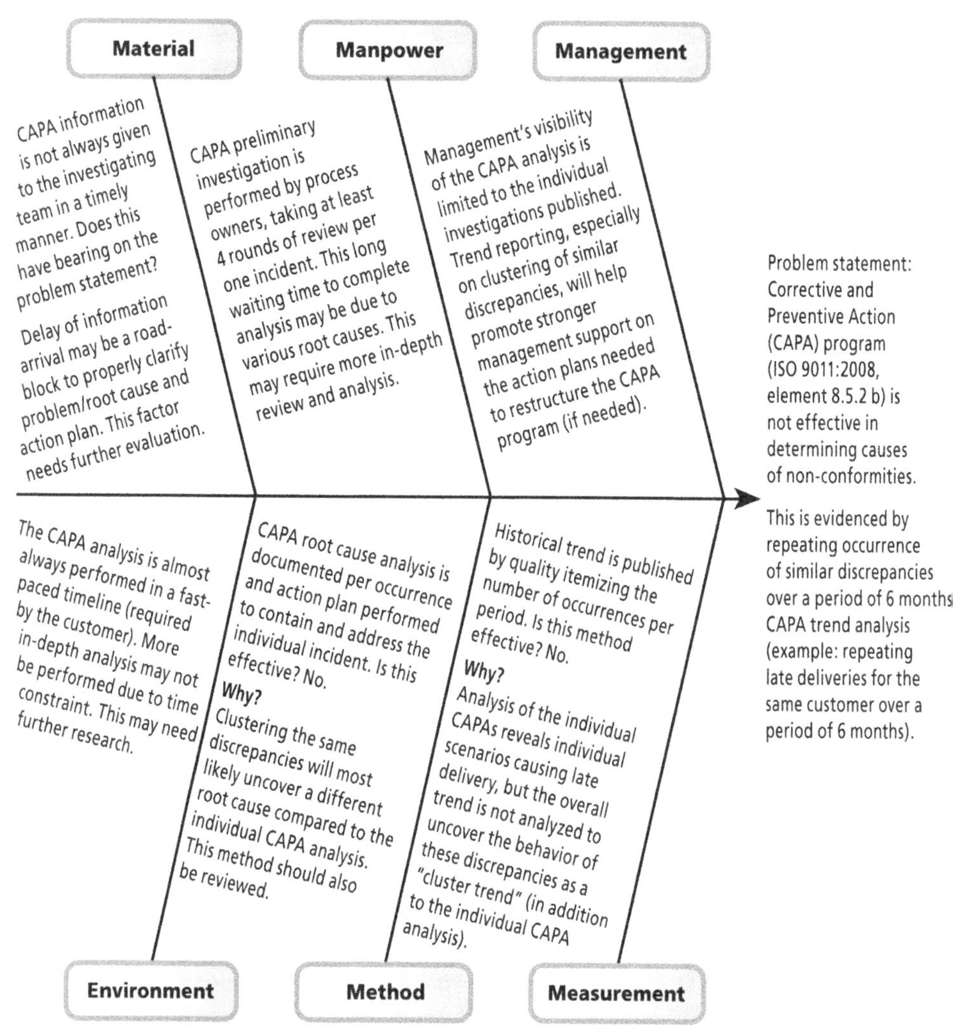

Figure 6.7 Analysis of corrective and preventive action effectiveness using fishbone diagram.

5 WHYS

Asking "why?" repeatedly (drilling down) will help uncover the root causes of a problem buried under a mass of information (see Figure 6.8). This tool helps reveal causes that are not easily visible, just like the hidden mass underneath the tip of the iceberg. Investigations often point to the easiest target (such as "operator error" or "it's a training issue"). This is a faulty assessment. There is almost always a reason for the operator error and this reason may be masked by noises louder than the voice of the operator. More and more organizations are recognizing this dilemma and using LSS tools and deeper analysis to determine true root causes so appropriate actions can be implemented.

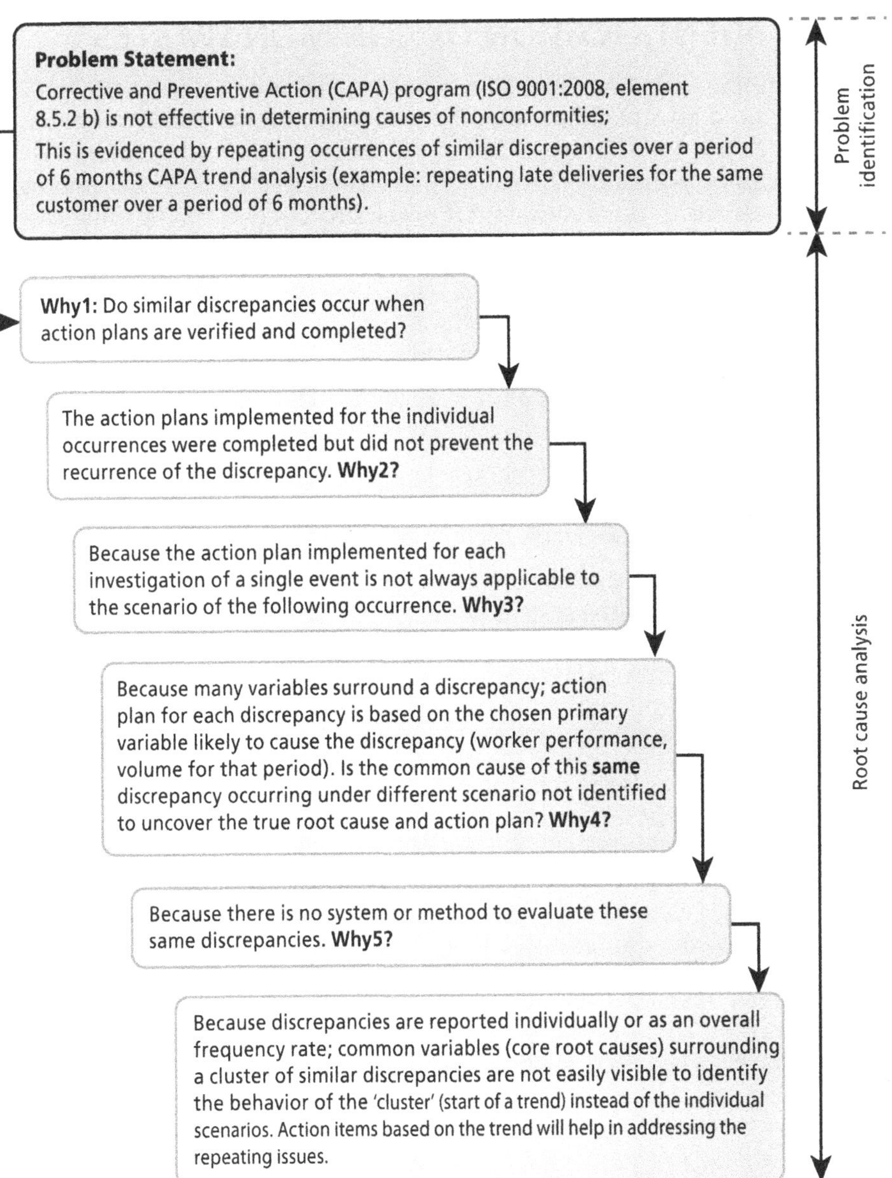

Problem Statement:
Corrective and Preventive Action (CAPA) program (ISO 9001:2008, element 8.5.2 b) is not effective in determining causes of nonconformities;
This is evidenced by repeating occurrences of similar discrepancies over a period of 6 months CAPA trend analysis (example: repeating late deliveries for the same customer over a period of 6 months).
Problem identification
Why1: Do similar discrepancies occur when action plans are verified and completed?
The action plans implemented for the individual occurrences were completed but did not prevent the recurrence of the discrepancy. Why2?
Because the action plan implemented for each investigation of a single event is not always applicable to the scenario of the following occurrence. Why3?
Because many variables surround a discrepancy; action plan for each discrepancy is based on the chosen primary variable likely to cause the discrepancy (worker performance, volume for that period). Is the common cause of this same discrepancy occurring under different scenario not identified to uncover the true root cause and action plan? Why4?
Because there is no system or method to evaluate these same discrepancies. Why5?
Because discrepancies are reported individually or as an overall frequency rate; common variables (core root causes) surrounding a cluster of similar discrepancies are not easily visible to identify the behavior of the 'cluster' (start of a trend) instead of the individual scenarios. Action items based on the trend will help in addressing the repeating issues.
Root cause analysis

Figure 6.8 5-Whys technique: evaluation of corrective and preventive action effectiveness.

IDENTIFICATION OF COMMON WASTES

Recognition and elimination of common wastes is an easy way to reduce variation and streamline the process. Auditing beyond compliance provides the opportunity to access this information during audits. This opportunity is an added value to the system, especially if the findings are measured in units meaningful to the process owners. In some cases waste, although in plain sight, is not easily visible to the workforce for the following possible reasons:

- Day-to-day encounter with waste makes it a familiar part of the environment; it goes unnoticed.
- Workers may have pointed out waste in the past, but if management takes no action, waste becomes the status quo.
- Waste may not be recognizable; it may appear in a form not easily associated with its original form. Its residual effect may be more visible than the waste itself.
- In some cases wastes are intentionally "hidden" to avoid jeopardizing the system (for example, sub-optimization of skills to benefit from the high performance of an overqualified worker through the manipulation of project assignment directly associated with the department in power, thus sub-optimizing other areas by depleting them of the qualified skills).
- Waste may be an inevitable part of the process and management may accept this as a lesser risk than addressing the waste. An example of this is the sorting performed by some companies on a very low-risk defect with low occurrence. It may be more economical to do a visual inspection and segregate non-conforming units rather than change the process.

The above scenarios highlight just a few of the many reasons for the existence of waste in the system. Regardless of its origin, waste is an element that requires attention so it can be properly managed. Not knowing its sources, severity, and impact on the business may cause serious revenue loss in the long run. Discovering waste at an early stage will permit proper mitigation before it has a major impact on the business. (See Figure 6.9.)

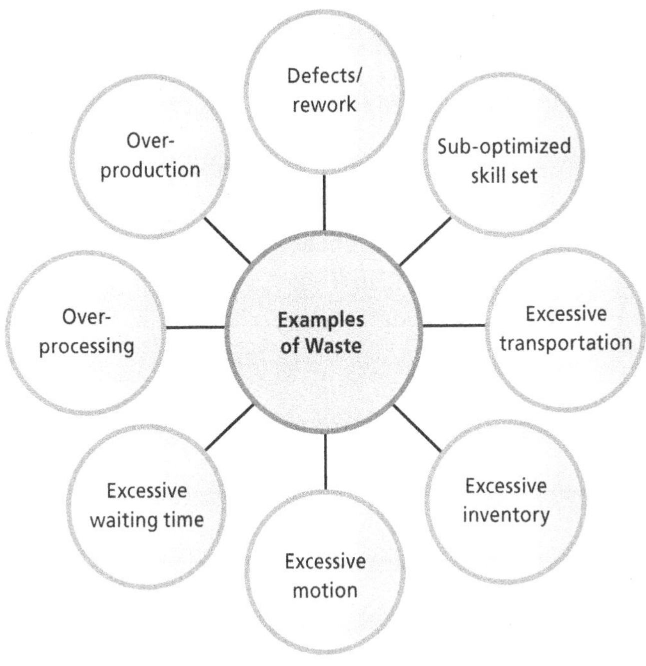

Figure 6.9 Examples of common wastes.

Reference: http://en.wikipedia.org/wiki/Muda_(Japanese_term) – Wastes identified by Toyota's Chief Engineer, Taiichi Ohno as part of the Toyota Production System

PARETO CHART ANALYSIS OF THE VITAL FEW

Ranking the elements being audited is a method of pre-selecting the "vital few from the trivial many." The vital few are likely to have greater consequence on the system and merit more focus and priority. This strategy has many associated consequences and side effects; caution is important if this route is practical for the application under evaluation. Once that decision is reached, the Pareto chart can be used as a visual aid to choose the vital few. This selection process depends on the integration of the company mission into the backbone of the system; it must be drilled down to the audit program. This philosophy will be the guiding force in choosing the vital few; it's based on, but not limited to, the following indicators:

- Frequency of occurrence
- Error rate/yield
- Safety risk level
- Customer acceptance or market demand
- Financial impact

Because the Pareto chart is a simple frequency graph of these variables, the selection process will be quantitative rather than subjective, as shown in Figure 6.10 (customer complaints by product code).

Selecting the vital few (if applicable) provides the following benefits:

- Vital items can be prioritized to optimize limited resources.
- High-risk items can be prioritized for containment and mitigation.
- Financial impact can be minimized through the timely identification of possible profit loss.
- Business can grow through the realization of major cost/profit drivers.

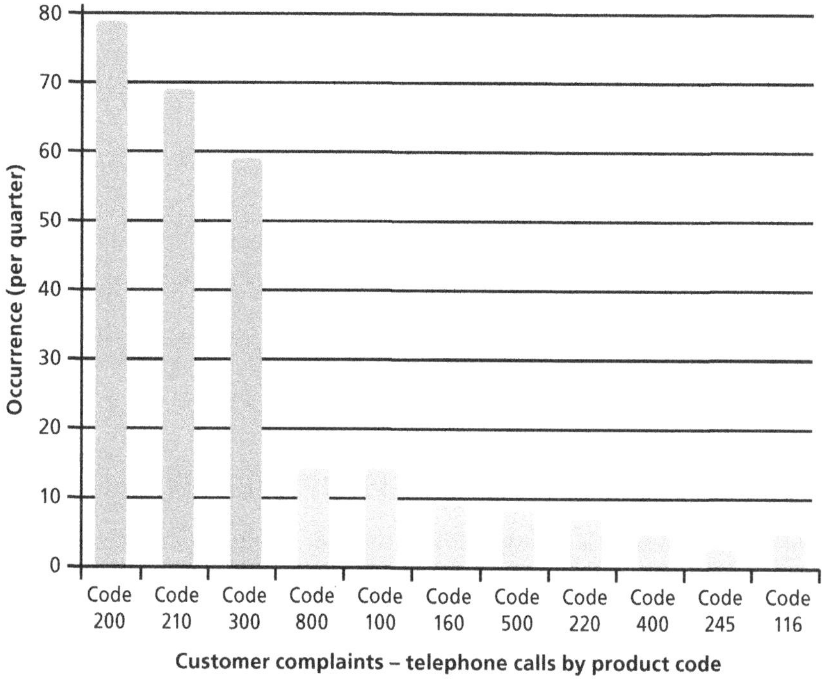

Figure 6.10 Pareto chart example 1: the vital few.

Pareto charts are a flexible analysis tool useful for viewing the primary variable behavior against a reference coordinate (for example, defect rate by product). This fascinating view of the variable's reactions to selected reference points (for example, claims rate changes by region, by customer, or by season) provides a deeper comprehension of the data integration system. Understanding data correlation will help optimize the different options associated with this initiative.

In Figure 6.10, trend of customer complaints by product code, we see that product codes 200, 210, and 300 have the highest complaints in comparison with the other product codes during the quarter under evaluation. This information seems to indicate that these three products may be the most problematic. Choosing another reference point such as sales volume might paint an entirely different picture. We might see that these three products have achieved the highest sale nationwide in comparison with the remaining product codes. In this case, the complaint/sales ratio would tell us that these three products are profit generators with relatively few complaints. Lesson learned: every coin has two sides. Data on a Pareto chart can be interpreted in more than one way; therefore, careful planning and selection of variables for Pareto analysis are essential to achieve meaningful data analysis, which is key to auditing beyond compliance.

Identification of the vital few requires recognition of the indicator associated with the issue under evaluation because the "appearance" of the vital few may take an unfamiliar form.

> **Example:** A combined rejection rate for four major products is displayed in the operations floor. The auditor was pleased to see that the defect rate was trending down; therefore, no observation was noted for this process. Because the chart did not show the breakdown of each product's rejection rate (which is critical to customer satisfaction), the auditor missed an opportunity. Although the overall rejection rate may serve a purpose, it does not show the quality performance of each product; thus, there is no measurement of individual product ratings or trends. Auditing beyond compliance will uncover hidden opportunities for improvement.

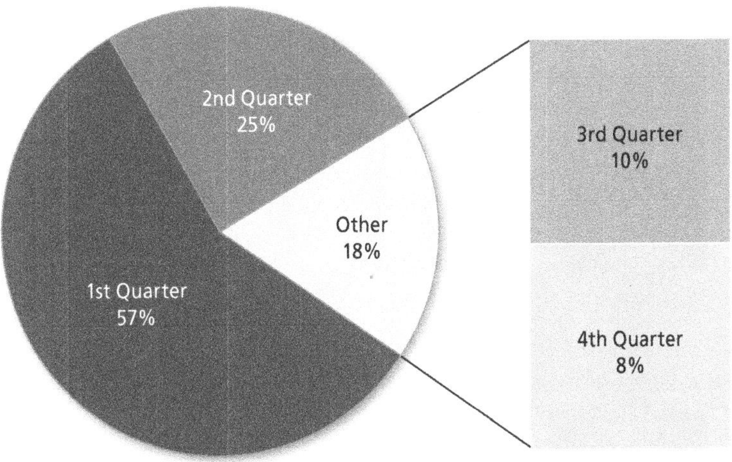

Figure 6.11 Pareto chart example 2: total rejection rate of products A, B, C, and D.

CRITICAL-TO-QUALITY (CTQ) METRICS

Problem: Batches of sterilized intraocular lenses in sealed pouches inside carton boxes were being rejected randomly by an overseas customer due to "dirty packaging" reported by the hospital (end-user). The hospital's policy was to return the entire batch to the manufacturer if any dirty units are found in the batch.

Upon return to the U.S. manufacturer, no evidence of dirty packaging was found; manufacturer assumed that whatever dirt was on the packaging had fallen off during shipment. No details could be obtained from the end users to help focus on the issue.

This complaint continued for several more batches, until the manufacturer sent an auditor overseas to verify conditions of stock storage and handling with the hope of finding the source of dirty packaging being reported by the hospital end user.

Observation: In this audit, the 6Ms of fishbone analysis were used to investigate and eliminate each element and to ultimately find the culprit.

As the evaluation of these 6Ms went on (for example, Method of storage handling, Machinery to transport the product within the hospital floors), no discrepancies were found until the Manpower interaction was verified. During the audit, the nurse retrieving the lenses from the stock room was observed looking intently at the outer packaging containing the sealed sterilized lens pouches and then segregating some boxes categorized as "dirty." The entire batch was pulled off the shelf for return to the manufacturer.

Conclusion: The outer boxes are manufactured from recycled corrugated material that shows some black specks or impurities embedded as part the recycling feature. Although the outer boxes have nothing to do with the product sterility, the nurse perceives these specks as signs of contamination.

This critical-to-quality customer perception was not considered when the product was marketed to this country and to the end users (hospitals). The culture places a different value on the overall cosmetic impact, something that should have been uncovered during the initial product introduction.

Action: Manufacturer agreed to use a different box material for this customer base. CTQ has been re-evaluated in Figure 6.12, CTQ analysis.

VOC (Voice of the Customer) – Issue:
The customer requirements in the scenario described in Figure 6.12 was also analyzed using the CTQ (critical-to-quality) identification to ensure the incoming and outgoing variables includes cosmetic requirements as part of the acceptance criteria for this customer.

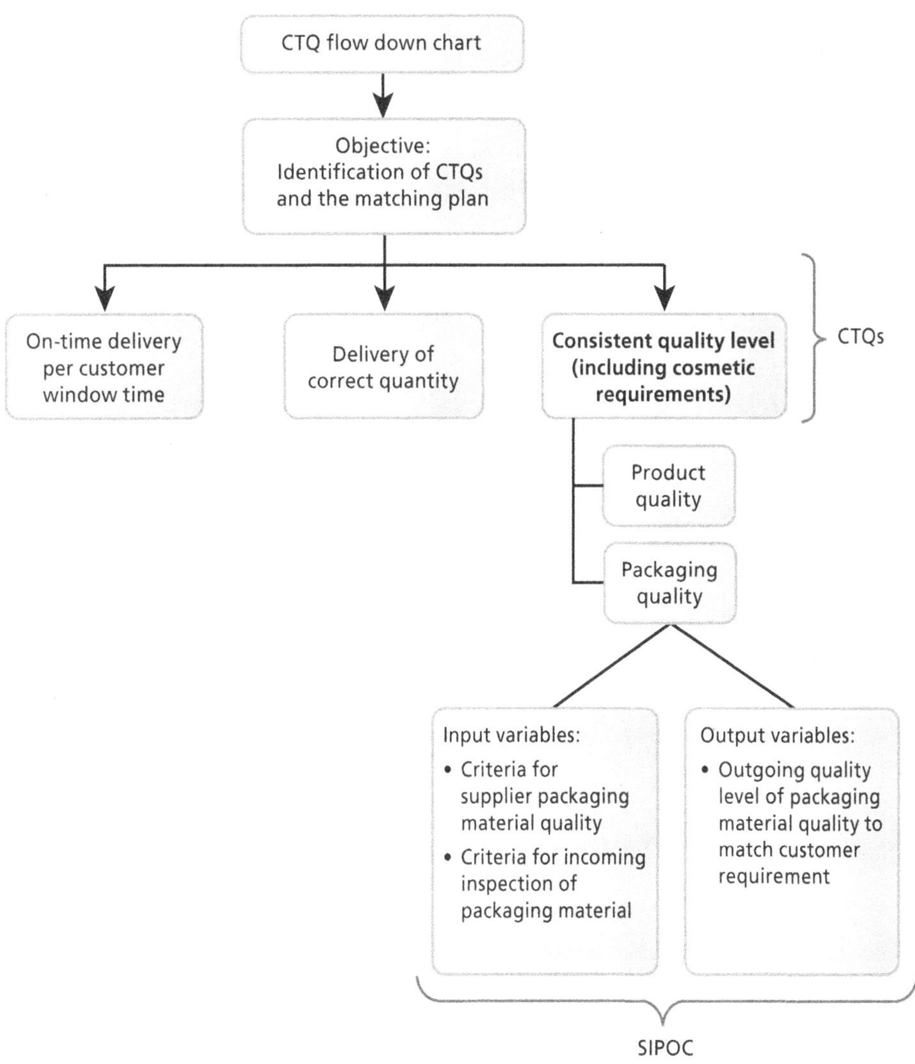

Figure 6.12 CTQ (critical-to-quality) metrics: customer perception.

7

Typical LSS Measures of Success

Completion of a task or action plan does not necessarily guarantee effectiveness of the plan. As an example, verifying completion of a procedure to address the inconsistent execution of a task does not qualify as sufficient verification of the action plan's effectiveness. Of course, one can spend hours or days to observe all the process owners executing the task as required by the written procedure to verify consistency, but this is too time consuming and expensive and it may not be physically possible (due to time constraint, security/safety issue restrictions, and so on). What is the next best option? Choosing a measure of success that will demonstrate effectiveness of the action taken will be more practical and a more efficient strategy in lieu of the first alternative. In this particular example, several measures of success (metrics) compared before and after the action plan's implementation will reflect the action plan's effectiveness. Examples include:

- Process yield or error rate
- Scrap/volume ratio
- Cycle time to complete the process per unit of measure
- Productivity or efficiency
- Customer satisfaction (for example, customer concern rate)

These measurable deliverables eliminate the subjectivity of the action plan's audit verification phase. This strategy also provides a benchmark for the next level; that is, the improvement phase triggered by auditing beyond compliance.

EFFECTIVE MEASUREMENTS OF SUCCESS

The Portable Universal Quality System (PUQL) model targets to exceed the expectations of auditing beyond compliance. The model serves as a collaborative plan for driving improvement and not just the removal of an influential data set that appears to be an outlier. This method widens the chances of missing the residual effect of variables that appear random but have significant impact on the overall behavioral trend of information clusters. This scenario is just one of the many "twists and turns" that should be considered in verifying the effectiveness of an action plan. An audit finding action plan offers a window to the cross-section of the system, a kaleidoscopic view revealing other patterns within the data set typically invisible or in plain sight but not noticed. Why? Typical audit design focused only on compliance may not have the detection mechanism built in to assess significant behavioral trends of data surrounding the compliance target (such as auditing beyond compliance). Thus, the PUQL model advocates the methodology of revealing associated variables and their impact to the entire system under evaluation. Each major variable, if uncovered, will facilitate recognition of the variable's connectivity strength and influence on the primary target of compliance. Recognizing influential factors is the first challenge.

The second challenge is defining the strength of connectivity these variables have to the compliance target. Each influential factor, as an entity or combined with the other variables, may cause a residual effect that cannot be ignored because it may prevent hitting the compliance target and improvement opportunities. Figure 7.1 is a visual depiction of the successful application of this strategy.

Achievement of audit compliance target (as depicted in Figure 7.1) is supported by the PUQL model designed to help capture data behavioral patterns not obvious with ordinary compliance auditing. The influential factors depicted in Figure 7.1 are also the measurement of success required in the PUQL audit model. It may be challenging for some auditors experienced in an environment highly focused solely on compliance verification to deviate from that structure. It is challenging but not impossible, especially if the system has committed to converting into auditing beyond compliance.

Like the bow and arrow sports, hitting the audit compliance target is affected by influential factors (observable and invisible) such as the following:

- Wind/lighting (process parameters)
- Type of equipment (customer requirement)
- Shooter's skill (workforce training)
- Distance (process yield)

Before adjustment of influential factors

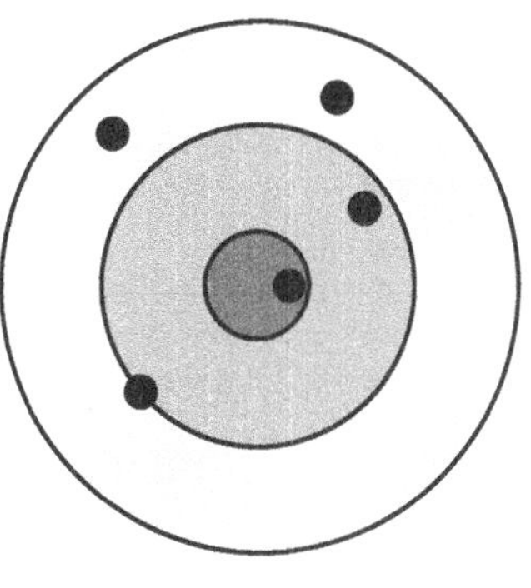

Adjustments can only be made if the influential factors are identified, measured, assessed, and then adjusted. Multiple adjustments may be needed.

Verification of success using this method is measurable and repeatable.

After adjustment of influential factors

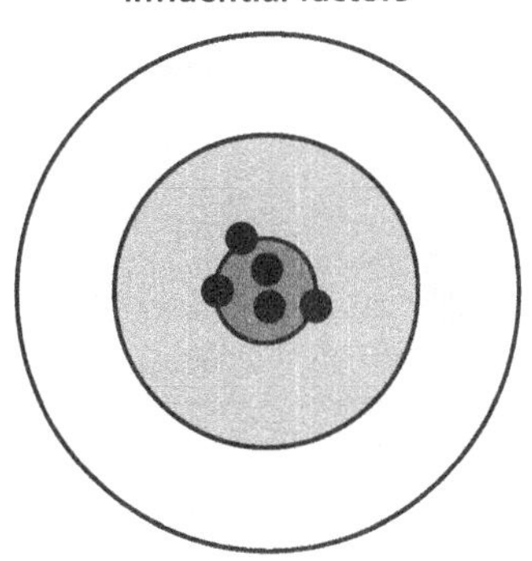

Figure 7.1 Audit compliance target (with measurement of success).

INCONSPICUOUS, DIFFICULT-TO-OBTAIN DELIVERABLES

Measurable deliverables associated with the action plan being verified sometimes are not conspicuous or easy to obtain. In this situation, indirect measurements may be considered to create a transfer of equivalent measurement from one format to another. This technique has been used since ancient times (for example, measuring the height of a pyramid by using the ratio of its shadow length measurement—easier to measure than the actual pyramid height—and an accessible reference such as a person's height and shadow length). A similar concept may be applied in auditing inaccessible direct measurements of success.

Below are examples of typical measurements of success in verifying effectiveness of action plans beyond compliance. The purpose of this matrix (Table 7.1) is to illustrate augmentation of conventional audit findings with measurable metrics commonly present in the system that can be plugged in the PUQL model.

Table 7.1 Measurements of success.

Typical action plan under traditional audit (without measurement of success)	Examples of Lean Measurement of Success (measurement of variation before and after action plan)
Training mitigation.	**Effectiveness** of training: • **Error rate %** • **Cycle time**
Improve resource allocation to meet demand.	• **Waiting time** • **Percent of on-time delivery** • **Unit level of effort** (work output per resource)
Restructure customer service to provide timely processing of customer changes.	• **Rate of customer follow up** (minimum follow up is desired) • **Processing time**
Reinforce training of material handling.	• **Damage rate** (caused by internal process) • **Customer claims** pertaining to internal process
Ensure implementation of customer requirement; improvement of Security Seal storage and accountability.	• **Inventory accuracy** • **Accessibility** (Note: Improvement of one element such as storage integrity should not jeopardize other elements such as accessibility, waiting time, and so on necessary to meet overall stakeholder requirements; otherwise, solution to one problem may create another issue).
Improve timeliness of response to customer inquiry.	• **Internal follow up** needed before completion of internal evaluation • **Cycle time** to process customer inquiry (upon receipt-to-completion) • **Customer complaints** regarding this issue

(Continued)

(Continued)

Table 7.1 Measurements of success.

Typical action plan under traditional audit (without measurement of success)	Examples of Lean Measurement of Success (measurement of variation before and after action plan)
Improve control over outsourced process to ensure conformity to customer/ regulatory requirements.	• **Time study** of cycle time (does the change impact on-time delivery?) • **Error rate** • **Waiting time** of next process • **Savings** if outsource was decided due to pure cost (outsource cost versus internal processing); this may be an input to identify waste, error rates, or streamlining opportunities to internal processing. Audit may not necessarily perform the savings analysis but can be identified during the review of the core processes.
Improve control of non-conforming product (OS&D: overage, shortage, and damage) to prevent mix-up.	• **Dwell time or inventory movement** rate of non-conforming material (this is one indication of the resolution rate of non-conforming material). • **Frequency rate** of mixed up materials originating in OS&D
Improve initiatives to ensure control of design and development software changes.	• **Coverage of all task** performance before and after software changes • **Cycle time** (to ensure resource management and on-time completion are maintained) • **Performance level**
Improve effectiveness of the management review input for visibility of recommendations for improvement.	• **Number of completed improvement** projects resulting from the management review input • **Percentage** of improvement projects **meeting target goal** (If projects are not meeting targets, this may be an indication that the improvement program is not effectively designed)
Ensure compliance to internal work instruction on dock check to ensure correct movement of freight.	• **Error and volume** ratio pertaining to this task (error rate alone will not accurately show progress as this element is affected by volume) • **Resource and volume ratio** (correct and timely movement of freight are affected by resource per volume allocation)

(Continued)

(Continued)

Table 7.1 Measurements of success.

Typical action plan under traditional audit (without measurement of success)	Examples of Lean Measurement of Success (measurement of variation before and after action plan)
Improve preventive maintenance cycle time to minimize downtime of machines.	• **Cycle time** • **Unplanned maintenance rate** (this information provides input on the effectiveness of preventive maintenance; preventive maintenance frequency may be adjusted based on the rate) • **Downtime**
Ensure preservation of freight during internal processing and delivery to maintain conformity to customer requirements.	• **Damage rate** (internal-controlled and supplier-controlled variables should be captured to identify causes of problems and effectiveness of internal controls)
Ensure effectiveness of software changes prior to production release.	Compare before and after the change: • **Task cycle time** affected by change • **Error rate** of task affected by change • **Productivity of workforce** performing task affected by change
Improve identification of customer requirements prior to contact acceptance.	• **Contract agreement completion rate** • **Error rate or customer complaint rate** on non-compliance (for example, shipping release documentation requirements)
Improve the efficiency of incoming materials delivery.	• **On-time delivery rate** • **Waiting time of delivery trailers** upon arrival at dock • **Unloading cycle time vs. manpower required** • **Cycle time to receive incoming materials-to-point of release** for production use
Improve retrieval of documents from central electronic archive by users.	• **Sample users and note successful retrieval rate and length of document search**
Improve project selection to maximize resource utilization.	Project selection success measurements: • **Savings** generated by the project • **Error rate** (if applicable) reduced by the improvement • **Process streamlining** (for example, reduction in labor hours and steps)

(Continued)

(Continued)

Table 7.1 Measurements of success.

Typical action plan under traditional audit (without measurement of success)	Examples of Lean Measurement of Success (measurement of variation before and after action plan)
Improve physical layout of area to streamline process.	• **Savings on unit level of effort** (for example, movement of manpower, equipment, information, and product) • **Error rate reduction** (if applicable)
Improve assembly process to meet on-time customer requirement.	• **On-time delivery** • **Overtime** • **Error rate** • **Productivity** • **Cost per unit** These metrics also measure cost that may be affected by the requirement versus the return of investment.
Improve supplier quality through supplier development program.	• **Incoming material quality level** • **Incoming inspection cost** • **Rejection rate**
Improve internal communication to increase awareness of the workforce on major changes affecting their processes.	• **Frequency of communication method** • **Awareness level of workforce**
Optimize sales department travel expenses to equate to "account win."	• **Ratio of sales expenses** versus account revenue contribution
Increase customer service support to customer telephone inquiries.	• **Cycle time** to resolve an issue per account • **Number of telephone calls** to resolve an issue • **Number of resolved issues** per customer service
Improve layout of warehouse to maximize freight movement.	• **Forklift mileage** versus weight of freight moved • **Forklift fuel consumption rate**
Improve the accuracy of the Phototool process for clean, clear images.	• **Number of rejected material** • **Cycle time** • **Rework rate**

(Continued)

(Continued)

Table 7.1 Measurements of success.

Typical action plan under traditional audit (without measurement of success)	Examples of Lean Measurement of Success (measurement of variation before and after action plan)
Improve accuracy of the first article inspection to prevent delays.	• **First article rate** • **In-process and final inspection rejection rate** • **Rework rate** • **Material requisition rate** • **Cycle time compared to standard** • **On-time delivery**

PUQL CHANGE VALIDATION

In addition to its use with the typical audit categories (product, process, and system), the PUQL model can be an innovative tool for the change management program. Key process indicators (KPIs) established for core processes require periodic audits to ensure the continuing equilibrium of the system. The primary purpose of periodic PUQL model audits is not to replace the operational day-to-day review of these KPIs as planning tools; rather, these audits are an overall assessment of the general direction of these initiatives. This will ensure alignment with the company mission. Change is almost constant for some companies; this may be simple to do or a complex task depending on the required change. An equilibrium point must be continually monitored to ensure the balance of "forces" within the system (such as customer demand and stakeholder risk). The PUQL template can function as a "quick" thermometer to detect or assess the initial impact of the change. It can be a rapid-response mechanism that can signal the system for further action. This concept is depicted in Figure 7.2 – detection of change as preventive control.

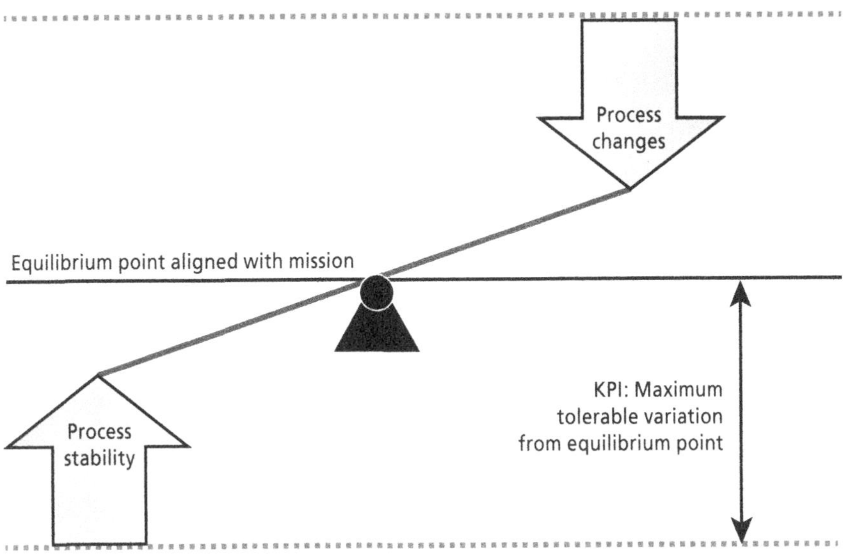

Figure 7.2 Detection of change as preventive control. (PUQL audit template can be used for this initiative.)

8

Identification of Wastes

The scope of Lean-Six Sigma processes is not limited to the promotion of continuous improvement; use of this initiative also strengthens the compliance aspect of any system. Improvement efforts are not necessarily technical or complex; some initiatives may be as simple as streamlining a process through the identification and minimization of day-to-day waste. Waste is a natural deterrent of progress and contributes to the unproductive process noise that distracts focus from the achievement of optimum process performance and/or compliance to standards. The existence of waste dilutes the system's effectiveness in maximizing the available resources to the fullest potential. Waste cannot be totally eliminated, but it can be controlled or contained to maintain an acceptable level. How can this program (that is, management of waste) be successfully achieved?

The first step is the recognition and identification of waste during audits. Identification of non-added-value variables (such as waste) interfering with the completion of an effective and efficient process will not be a difficult task during an audit. Awareness of associated wastes applicable to the product, process, or system under evaluation will help uncover these non-added value items. Another strategy is to ask this question: "What will prevent you from accomplishing your assigned tasks?" This simple question, in most cases, will help the auditor identify wastes or roadblocks that prevent process owners from achieving their goals.

Auditing (whether system, process, or product) is a golden opportunity to observe wastes that will trigger improvement opportunity and detect compliance issues. Noting wastes during audits is an example of auditing beyond compliance.

Table 8.1 lists typical examples of observable wastes and how these wastes impact not only productivity and efficiency but also compliance.

Severity of the wastes may be identified by quantifying in terms of appropriate unit of measure (for example: wasted approximately 30 minutes for each incoming material by opening boxes to search for packing slips; occurrence is approximately 10 times per week or approximately 5 hours total wasted time per week).

Table 8.1 Examples of observable wastes, and the correlation between inefficiency and non-compliance.

Examples of observable wastes	Signs of inefficiency and/or compliance issues
Excessive walking to make copies of paperwork needed for task completion.	**Process layout:** Needs improvement to make equipment/paperwork more accessible to users. **Possible impact on compliance:** Unnecessary fatigue may cause error and possible mix-up of paperwork.
Waiting time to receive incoming material due to missing paperwork.	**Supplier development:** Supplier must improve service quality (such as complete traceability/ paperwork with every shipment) **Possible impact on compliance:** Traceability issue.
Extra movement and processing/labeling of non-conforming materials out of the dock for segregation until issue is resolved.	**Supplier performance** monitoring needs more visibility to ensure monitoring of supplier performance quality. **Possible impact on compliance:** Multiple handling of material may cause damage or potential mix-up.
Double handling of materials already loaded on trailers but unloaded due to last-minute customer change.	**Change management** not effective in controlling parameters such as signed cut-off time on customer changes. **Possible impact on compliance:** Multiple handling of material may cause damage or possible mix-up (traceability issue).
High material damage rate during forklift loading of materials recorded in Damage Log in comparison with previous periods, causing upward trending rate of claims.	**Ineffective training** of new material handlers assigned to task being observed. **Possible impact on compliance:** Customer satisfaction requirements are not consistently met.

(Continued)

(Continued)

Table 8.1 Examples of observable wastes, and the correlation between inefficiency and non-compliance.

Examples of observable wastes	Signs of inefficiency and/or compliance issues
High maintenance cost of forklift tires for one warehouse in comparison with other warehouses.	**Infrastructure/facility maintenance plan** not effective to identify irregular ramp surface at loading dock snagging the forklift tires causing tire damage. **Possible impact on compliance:** Forklift downtime may ultimately affect on-time processing or on-time delivery.
Multiple document changes for one process (in comparison with other processes shown on revision log) within short period interval. These multiple changes cause training and re-training of process owners, possible waste.	**Validation of process** may require re-evaluation of hand-off deliverables. Multiple changes within short period of time are not against regulation, but may be a symptom of process instability or poor acceptance criteria. **Possible impact on compliance:** Unstable process creates variation that may impact customer satisfaction.
Over-processing of a typical late delivery freight complaint; one completed report involved 20 people, 100 internal email messages prior to completion of the analysis. This timeframe for completing a standard 8-D report was found typical in processing a single complaint as shown in 10 samples.	**Failure Mode Effect Analysis program (FMEA)** does not seem to be effective in providing quick reference to failure mode analysis/action plans. Typical failures likely to occur in the industry should be covered in the company's FMEA program as part of the analysis tool. Investigation/review team and data-mining methodology may require re-evaluation to streamline the process. **Possible impact on compliance:** True root cause may not be easily uncovered under existing system; therefore, corrective action may not always be effective.
Over-process of information: information transferred in different formats for dissemination to different customers.	**No work instruction** to standardize outgoing reports; because there is no standard format, customers designed their own formats, which means customer service representatives create multiple reports for the same information. **Possible impact on compliance:** Non-standardized documentation will likely generate error during data transfer.

(Continued)

(Continued)

Table 8.1 Examples of observable wastes, and the correlation between inefficiency and non-compliance.

Examples of observable wastes	Signs of inefficiency and/or compliance issues
Overtime: Audit of the off-shift noted the same operators. Operators stated that they have been doing overtime for more than a month to cover for the off-shift, although there is no change in volume being processed. A change in the supplier's process caused the delivery of materials during off shift. Since there is no volume change, no additional resource can be added to cover the off-shift, thus the overtime.	**Human resource allocation** may not be effective in matching peak workload and resource assignment (for example, staggering of schedules to cover all shifts instead of overtime). **Contract agreement** with supplier may need to be re-evaluated to include advance notification of significant changes, for example, window time of deliveries, and so on. **Possible impact on compliance:** Unbalanced resource allocation may ultimately affect proper support of the process at the expected performance.
A pile of suspect materials pending resolution for approximately 3 months, a waste of time/material and space.	**Acceptance criteria** may require clarification to provide concise guidelines for the evaluation of material (such as use of visual aids). Material review should also have a timeline for completion of resolution. **Possible impact on compliance:** Possible mix-up that may affect traceability; multiple handling of material may cause damage (impact on customer satisfaction).
Repeating error/defect noted in customer complaint trend.	**Root cause analysis** may not be effective, therefore actions taken are not effective in preventing recurrence of errors. **Possible impact on compliance:** Customer dissatisfaction.
Volumes of paperwork reviewed to find needed quality record as observed during audit. (Waste of time, energy, and space.)	**Generation of paper** copies may require re-evaluation to determine if electronic records are applicable to replace hard copies as quality records. This will also improve accessibility and archiving system. **Possible impact on compliance:** This may impact traceability.

(Continued)

(Continued)

Table 8.1 Examples of observable wastes, and the correlation between inefficiency and non-compliance.

Examples of observable wastes	Signs of inefficiency and/or compliance issues
Under-utilized resource: Cleaning crew was observed cleaning bathrooms multiple times during the audit.	**With the implementation of 5S system,** the operations workforce maintains a cleaner and more organized environment, reducing the need for cleaning crew. Cleaning crew fills idle time with busy work. Management should review resource allocation to address this issue. **Possible impact on compliance:** Improper resource planning and utilization definitely impacts process performance necessary to support all aspect of the operations to consistently achieve customer satisfaction.
Ineffective/wasteful auditing practice: A customer audit (second party audit) stated "lack of written procedures" based on one operator failing to identify the form for a particular task.	**This particular scenario illustrates several wastes:** The customer auditor (second party audit) required a management audience to use this single sample as a conclusion evidence on the integrity of the auditee's total documentation system. A single sample is not necessarily a conclusive representation of the total quality system; additional samples may be needed to provide a more accurate conclusion. **Possible impact on compliance:** Ineffective audit feedback does not correct issues but only adds to process noise. **What action can be recommended, as this is a sensitive matter, such as customer (second party) audit?** The company being audited should have an open dialogue with the customer auditor to evaluate the logic of the auditor's perception formed based on a singular observation during the audit. Typically, a singular incident is not a representation of the total system breakdown; therefore, the conclusion made by the customer auditor may have an underlying reason. Customer perception is important and may have a bearing on the business relationship; therefore, appropriate consideration should be given as needed.

(Continued)

(Continued)

Table 8.1 Examples of observable wastes, and the correlation between inefficiency and non-compliance.

Examples of observable wastes	Signs of inefficiency and/or compliance issues
Wasted audit question: Customer auditor (second party) asked this question: "Why do you do a gap analysis when you just told us that your company is compliant?"	**Skill set may not be matching required responsibility:** The auditor's question showed lack of insight on the true meaning of gap analysis. Gap analysis is a dynamic process and should be continued to ensure that ever-changing variables (for example, changes in volume, schedule, customer-base, and so on) are not impacting the system's effectiveness. Compliant process may be stable now, but ongoing changes may cause variation; performance of gap analysis must be ongoing to ensure continuing performance level. **Possible impact on compliance:** The skill set of the audit function needs to be properly aligned with the assigned mission; otherwise, the audit function will not be effective. Different audit hierarchy will require different levels of training and qualification. Simple in-process visual audit (for example, sorting broken bags of candies on a running conveyor) requires a skill set different from a quality system audit of a business partner.

9

Other Lean-Based Audit Report Formats

Audit report formats will vary according to requestor expectations. No single magic formula will satisfy everyone. It is therefore important to keep in mind that the report should reflect, at minimum, the following elements:

- **Purpose** – What is the reason for this report? Is it for an executive summary requiring only high level update, or is it for a technical review that requires more details and statistical analysis?
- **Expectations of the reader** – Is the reader expecting simplified information in graphs for easy viewing of trends or financial impact? Is the reader expecting the raw data to be available for review or just the summary?
- **Regulatory requirements** – Must certain reports be incorporated in the format?

Typical audit reports consist of elements such as these:

- Scope or purpose
- Standard or reference to be used as baseline
- Area/product/system under audit
- Audit findings
- Process owners' action plan and timeline
- Verification data

Reporting a Lean-Six Sigma-based audit beyond compliance includes additional elements not normally found in typical audits:

- LSS tools used by auditors for data mining or translating observed events into measurable findings
- Identification of waste and/or improvement opportunities that impact compliance in one way or another

- The financial impact of waste or inefficiencies that cause non-compliance
- Metrics to baseline and measure effectiveness of corrective actions

These additional elements may be considered by some LSS practitioners to be the "signature" of LSS-based audits.

Regardless of format the audit report must have a "special effect" that will capture the interest of the audit champion or stakeholder. That special effect will be dependent on the expectations and requirements of the champion who should have been identified at the beginning of the audit endeavor. The audit champion need not be an individual; the "champion" can be the customer requirement, reference standard, or regulatory requirement needed to maintain the business.

Understanding the expectations of the champion aligns the direction of the audit and the focus of the audit report. Since this publication highlights auditing beyond compliance, the audit report formats shown in the following pages are geared toward that direction. A typical auditor already has basic knowledge of a conventional audit report format (for example, ISO 9001); therefore, those audit report elements will not be shown in the following examples. The examples will focus on the additional elements that will be part of an LSS audit report.

AUDIT REPORT COVER SHEET

The Portable Universal Quality Lean audit template (PUQL) discussed in Chapter 5 may be sufficient as the final audit report for some application. In some cases, the audit champion (executive management or a regulatory body) may require a report summary cover sheet that includes certain information or a preferred format. The completed PUQL templates used during the audit may be attached to the audit report cover sheet accessible to the audit review team as needed (Figures 9.1–9.4). Another option is to use the PUQL template as part of the raw data sheet used for data mining the information. There are many options to consider; the ultimate decision maker is the report user or recipient.

> **Scenario:** A gap analysis was requested by management to determine the center's CTPAT compliance and readiness to apply for the CTPAT third-party audit. Note: CTPAT means Customs Trade Partnership Against Terrorism, sponsored by the Custom Border Patrol regulatory body.

Auditors:
Corporate – Director of Quality and Continuous Improvement
Local center – Director of Safety

Duration of the audit: February 27–March 2, 2012

Purpose:
Gap analysis of Center E to assess CTPAT regulation compliance based on requirements of CTPAT regulations manual CBP, revision X

Scope/Audit Methodology:
Center compliance was based on:
- Employee interviews and observation
- Sampling of records versus regulation requirement

Raw Data:
PUQL audit templates were completed for the different CTPAT elements; these are available for review as needed.

Executive Summary:
Strengths: The CTPAT elements are incorporated in the day-to-day operations as observed and detected through interviews .

Areas Needing Improvement:
Knowledge transfer is mostly verbal communication (tribal knowledge).

Figure 9.1 Audit report format, sample 1.

Product Audit Report

Team: **Date:**

Purpose/Problem: This gap analysis was triggered by the recent mix-up of part XXX, requiring rework and causing late delivery of PO# CCC. Approximate cost of error: $X to cover material replacement, labor, and shipping expedite.

Scope: The improvement plan in this report pertains to the processes depicted in the diagram below, using PO number CCC as source of information:

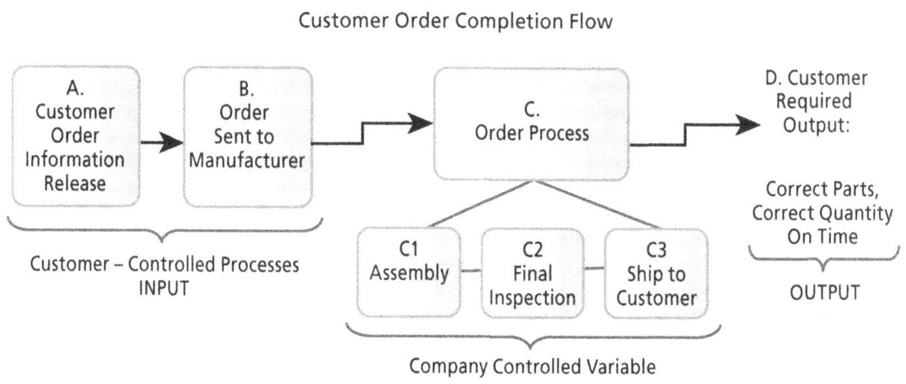

Evaluation Methodology: Gap analysis was based on process observation, interview of workers, product/process/record audit, and review of the recent customer complaint. SIPOC diagram was used to analyze the issue.

Overall Finding: Mix-up error occurred at Process A and B (customer-controlled variables). Parts and paperwork supplied by customer were mixed upon hand-off for Order Processing (Box C).

Root Causes: The error-proofing methodology for the customer-controlled processes need restructuring to increase its effectiveness at Process A and B.

There was no dynamic error prevention and/or early detection (if error occurs) at the hand-off process (Box C), thus, previous error was passed on to the next processes.

Plan	Measurement of Success
Process Flow Improvement Plan Electronic information will be sent during the hand-off at Process C for easy access and review. 5S program will be implemented to improve material organization and support error-proofing, for Process A-B and C. Responsibility: ____________ Timeline: ____________	**A. Process Metrics:** Progress of process performance will be monitored via first piece/set-up. A1. % order with non-conformance A2. % order with incomplete information from Process A and B (Error rate cost before and after action plan (downward trend = cost savings). **B. 5S savings:** ULE (unit level of effort) before and after the change, such as savings in movement and waiting time after 5S implementation

Verification: Follow up will be performed in 2 weeks to assess progress and effectiveness via metrics results.

Figure 9.2 Audit report format, sample 2.

Gap Analysis Report Date:________________
Purpose of Evaluation: Approximately 30% of incoming materials are held at Plant B, causing delay and expedite cost of $XX; period covered: XX to XX; Team will use SIPOC to analyze gaps. **Team:** XX

SIPOC Diagram
Supplier–Input–Process–Output–Customer Requirement

SUPPLIER/INPUT
Plant A
Raw Materials Flow
PROCESS/OUTPUT
Plant B
Task 1
Task 2
Task 3
Processed Material Flow
CUSTOMER REQUIREMENT
Plant C

Supplier/ Input	Process	Output / Customer Requirement	Possible root cause Action Plan / Responsibility / Timeline
Highlight: Material and Traceability information Plant A	**Highlight:** System restrictions cause data errors during material release	**Critical-to-Quality (CTQ):** 100% acceptance of material from Plants A-to-C **Gap 1:** Approximately 30% incoming materials are put "on hold" at Plant B due to data error coming from Plant A	**Possible root causes:** Material movement in system not synchronized with physical release. **Action:** IT department will be involved to synchronize system with physical movement. **Responsibility:** VV/Date XX
		CTQ: 100% damage-free material and proper stacking for easy unloading Plants A-to-C **Gap 2:** Some shipments are not loaded or stacked properly, causing carton damage after receipt from Plant A	**Possible root causes:** a. Improper stacking was traced back to handling practices; if no instruction is noted on boxes, boxes are assumed stackable. **Action:** Non-stackable boxes (containing fragile materials) will be labeled "Do Not Double Stack." **Responsibility:** VV/Date XX
		CTQ: Approval must occur prior to any change. **Gap 3:** Changes in shipping configuration not always communicated to Plant C.	**Root cause:** Some of the changes relayed are not in formal documentation. **Action:** Creation of Change Request form to document and route for approval of major changes. **Responsibility:** VV/Date XX

Figure 9.3 Audit report format, sample 3.

<table>
<tr><th colspan="5">Gap Analysis Report Format</th></tr>
<tr><td colspan="5">Purpose of Audit: Department X error rate and late deliveries are trending upward. This audit aims to find the root causes and determine action plans.
Scope: Period ___ to ___, Department XX
Team Members: Process owners will be responsible to complete action items on or before XX</td></tr>
<tr><th>Problem / Roadblock</th><th>Waste</th><th>Root Cause</th><th>Actions by Process Owners</th><th>Verification/ Measure of Success</th></tr>
<tr><td>Traceability issue due to lost Proof of Delivery required by customers.</td><td>Delay and wasted time.</td><td>Lack of archive process for easy retrieval of information</td><td>Organize/archive information by category (for example, by customer).</td><td>Unit level of effort and time before and after the action plan
Number of lost paperwork before and after action plan</td></tr>
<tr><td>Billing method is not efficient, causing XX cost in labor.</td><td>Current manual method is time consuming.</td><td>Billing paperwork is manual and cumbersome; prone to errors.</td><td>IT will be consulted for conversion of manual system into automated process.</td><td>Unit level of effort and time before and after the action plan</td></tr>
<tr><td>Misrouted freight</td><td>Potential misrouting if areas are not clearly marked (mix-up).</td><td>Quarantine areas are not currently marked.</td><td>Define areas and paint them.</td><td>Error rate before and after action plan</td></tr>
<tr><td>Late deliveries</td><td>Overtime and possible missing on-time deliveries if not properly managed.</td><td>Planning was not based on workload.</td><td>Develop a new schedule to better align resource and peak volume time.</td><td>Number of on-time deliveries before and after action plan
Overtime–volume ratio before and after action plan</td></tr>
</table>

Figure 9.4 Audit report format, sample 4.

PROJECT CHARTERS

The following pages are examples of project charters resulting from an audit finding using the PUQL template (see Figures 9.5 and 9.6). Combined with the LSS approach, the audit function has leverage for detecting not only compliance gaps but also improvement opportunities. These opportunities are not necessarily the responsibility of the Quality/Audit function; these roles depend on the organizational structure. The multi-functional teams responsible for the improvement portion of the operation will benefit from this detection mechanism, built-in within the PUQL concept and template system. Improvement opportunities may be a quick fix to a project requiring resources for completion. In the earlier chapters, we discussed that management and grassroots level buy-in plays a critical role in the success of this audit methodology. With this buy-in, it will be easier to "sell" the importance of the findings beyond compliance, which may require a more involved action plan and an LSS project. Through the application of the LSS approach, the project initiated by the PUQL concept/template will have measurable deliverables that will dictate the project's priority status. The project completion may be the action plan to address the audit finding.

Project management of Lean projects is a topic beyond the scope of this module; the following pages are just examples of the project charter. There are more steps after the audit finding before an initiative turns into a Lean project. That topic is also beyond the scope of this publication, but there are many reference books available for this endeavor.

Voice of the Project Champion		
"Customer's assembly system cycle time is longer than expected due to repeating order entry errors, a cumbersome order process, and long waiting time for parts release to the keep the assembly line optimized. There are wastes throughout the process that must be identified to improve efficiency."		
Problem Statement (Convert project champion's voice into clear problem statement, with measure of severity if possible)		
Current parts order entry for the line feed system has an error rate of 20%, causing a process waiting time of approximately 24 hours for each job completion.		
Project Goal or Deliverables		
The goal is to identify the primary causes of errors and delays and to: • reduce **error rate** to at least 10% or less • reduce current **cycle time** by at least 30%		
Project Scope		
This project will cover the following processes: Part Number (PN) Order Request → PN Order Entry → PN Release to Line Feed Time frame under evaluation: ________________		
Metrics to Measure Success		
	Primary Tasks List (not limited to the following):	Timeline/ Responsibility
	Create a value stream map	
	Validate cycle times through time study and observation of different shifts	
	Update value stream map/identify bottlenecks (to prioritize analysis)	
	Analyze root causes of bottlenecks; use Fishbone diagram (if needed, observe processes)	
	Select primary root causes from Fishbone diagram; focus on the vital few using Pareto analysis.	
	Team to analyze possible recommendations to address root causes	
	Perform risk assessment of feasible recommendations and associated benefits/costs.	
	Validate trial run of improvement plan; verify metrics against baseline.	
	Hand-off approval process	
Milestones/Timelines/Responsibilities		
Team Leader:	Champion:	Team Members:
Project Charter Approval:		

Figure 9.5 Sample project charter, assembly system.

Voice of the Project Champion

"Customer feedback program is not timely to show sense of urgency to customer inquiries or complaints. It takes a long time before a response is issued to the customer; in most cases, the action plans noted on the responses are not effective (as shown by recurrence of non-conformance)."

Problem Statement
(Convert project champion's voice into clear problem statement, with measure of severity if possible)

a. Cycle time for processing customer inquiries or complaints exceeds customer's tolerable waiting time (current cycle ranges from 10–30 days, average of 20 days).

b. Root cause analysis needs re-evaluation to verify effectiveness of action plans.

Project Goal or Deliverables

The goal is to identify the primary causes of delay, to measure the baseline for this process, and improve effectiveness of action plans:

- reduce **cycle time** by at least 50% or more (baseline: current cycle time)
- reduce **recurrence rate** of complaints by at least 50% (baseline: current recurrence rate of same non-conformance)

Project Scope

This project will cover the following processes:

External customer complaint period: ______________________

Metrics to Measure Success

Before and after improvement implementation:

- Cycle time
- Non-conformance trend (recurrence rate by category such as location, customer, and so on)
- Resource time allocated for investigation-to-completion of the customer response

Milestones/Timelines/Responsibilities

Primary Tasks List (not limited to the following):	Timeline/ Responsibility
Prepare value stream map to understand flow of process	
Identify roadblocks and analyze possible causes	
Select the vital few for prioritization	
Team to recommend improvement plan	
Risk analysis (cost vs. benefits)	
Validation of chosen plan	
Hand-off approval	

Team Members

Team Leader: Champion: Team Members:

Project Charter Approval:

Figure 9.6 Sample project charter: corrective action effectiveness and cycle time.

10

Avoiding an Untimely End

It is tragic to witness a well-designed program, such as an auditing beyond compliance initiative, fall into a sinkhole before it reaches optimum capability. Sadly, it can happen in a blink. Why?

Like a machine, any program has a life cycle affected by many variables leading to great success or failure. Early recognition of these potential pitfalls is critical in mitigating fall-out and turning crisis situations into positive and profitable process excellence events. Table 10.1 shows examples of auditing beyond compliance pitfalls and preventive action plans.

Table 10.1 Auditing beyond compliance pitfalls to avoid.

Pitfalls	Possible causes *(not limited to the following)*	How to detect, avoid, and/or mitigate
"Rocket booster" effect wherein program's life expectancy is bright but short lived; no sustenance.	• Program objectives not clearly defined	Confirm Involvement of both management and grassroots level in identifying objectives with timeline.
"Early death" or premature obsolescence.	• Over-engineering • Overly conservative approach that causes ideas to become obsolete even before launching the program	Project scope and methodology must be defined and approved by the users/team. This is to ensure balance of project management goals and timeline. **Example:** Simple use of tracking tool such as Gantt chart to ensure visibility of each phase.

(Continued)

Table 10.1 Auditing beyond compliance pitfalls to avoid.

Pitfalls	Possible causes *(not limited to the following)*	How to detect, avoid, and/or mitigate
"Rolling Stone Effect" wherein the scope, direction, and other core elements of the program are continually changed, creating a never-ending cycle of wasteful data-mining efforts without concrete results.	• Immaturity of the team's subject expertise or inadequate project management knowledge base • Silo effect	Re-evaluate initiative's team membership and clarify roles.
"Superstar Syndrome," wherein some areas are sub-optimized to support quick wins on low hanging fruit, giving a perception of quick success but providing no-long term benefit for the system.	• Team objectives not aligned with company mission	Initiatives or project selections should be approved by a multi-functional team to balance the scorecard.
"Low Hanging Fruit Syndrome," an initiative that, regardless of its solid design, will not add value if not aligned with management's vision.	• Silo environment • Lack of communication	Ensure management buy-in on key milestones to ensure alignment with business plan.
"Quicksand Platform Effect" Initiative start-up was well supported but enthusiasm was slowly overpowered by day-to-day priorities.	• Unbalanced resource allocation	Commitment of required resources and timelines must be visible to immediately prevent/detect roadblocks.
Cost of initiative exceeds ROI (return on investment).	• Poor planning and inadequate risk assessment	Primary cost drivers should be identified versus the chosen project cost indicators.
Output expectation exceeds program capability.	• Realistic expectations not set at the beginning of the initiative. • Lack of communication	Define expectations at the start of the program, with measurable deliverables.

(Continued)

(Continued)

Table 10.1 Auditing beyond compliance pitfalls to avoid.

Pitfalls	Possible causes *(not limited to the following)*	How to detect, avoid, and/or mitigate
Business cultural differences (management values vs. grassroots level buy-in).	• Grassroots level has not embraced the methodology to fully understand the value of the objectives. Without grassroots support, the Process Excellence platform will collapse.	Goals need to be re-assessed.

References

American National Standards Institute (ANSI), International Organization for Standardization (ISO), American Society for Quality (ASQ). ANSI/ISO/ASQ Q9001-2008, *Quality management system requirements.* 2008.

Bautista Smith, J. July 2010. "Rapid Response to Customer Complaints," *Quality Progress.* American Society for Quality.

CFR (Code of Federal Regulations) Title 21/Good Manufacturing Practices, Food and Drug Administration, Department of Health and Human Services.

Customs-Trade Partnership Against Terrorism (C-TPAT) Manual. 2010. U.S. Customs Border Patrol.

International Automotive Task Force and the Technical Committee of ISO. ISO/TS 16949:2009. *Quality management systems — Particular requirements for the application of ISO 9001:2008 for automotive production and relevant service part organizations.*

Juran, J.M. and A.B Godfrey. 1999. *Juran's Quality Handbook, 5th Edition,* New York-McGraw Hill.

Kubiak, T. M. and Donald W. Benbow. 2009. *The Certified Six Sigma Black Belt Handbook, 2nd Edition,* ASQ Quality Press.

Microsoft Products: SmartArt Graphic feature of Microsoft Office Word 2007, Microsoft Visio 2010 and Microsoft Excel 2007.

Munro, R., M. Maio, M. Nawaz, R. Govindarajan, and D. Zyrmiak. 2008. *The Certified Six Sigma Green Belt Book.* ASQ Quality Press.

Pyzdek, T. 2003. *The Six Sigma Handbook: A Complete Guide for Green Belts, Black Belts and Managers,* New York-McGraw Hill.

Society of Automotive Engineers and the European Association of Aerospace Industries. SAE T9100 Revision C: AS9100C Quality Management Systems — Aerospace Requirements. 2009.

TL 9000, QMS Requirements, Quest Forum.

U.S. Defense Logistics Agency. 1995. *MIL-PRF-31032 Standard for Printed Circuit Board/Printed Wiring Board,* Department of Defense.

Index

Page numbers in *italics* refer to figures and tables.

E

F

G

H

I-J

K

L

M

N

O

P

Q

R

S

ASQ Membership

Research shows that people who join associations experience increased job satisfaction, earn more, and are generally happier.* ASQ membership can help you achieve this while providing the tools you need to be successful in your industry and to distinguish yourself from your competition. So why wouldn't you want to be a part of ASQ?

Networking

Have the opportunity to meet, communicate, and collaborate with your peers within the quality community through conferences and local ASQ section meetings, ASQ forums or divisions, ASQ Communities of Quality discussion boards, and more.

Professional Development

Access a wide variety of professional development tools such as books, training, and certifications at a discounted price. Also, ASQ certifications and the ASQ Career Center help enhance your quality knowledge and take your career to the next level.

Solutions

Find answers to all your quality problems, big and small, with ASQ's Knowledge Center, mentoring program, various e-newsletters, *Quality Progress* magazine, and industry-specific products.

Access to Information

Learn classic and current quality principles and theories in ASQ's Quality Information Center (QIC), *ASQ Weekly* e-newsletter, and product offerings.

Advocacy Programs

ASQ helps create a better community, government, and world through initiatives that include social responsibility, Washington advocacy, and Community Good Works.

Visit www.asq.org/membership for more information on ASQ membership.

*2008, The William E. Smith Institute for Association Research

ASQ Certification

ASQ certification is formal recognition by ASQ that an individual has demonstrated a proficiency within, and comprehension of, a specified body of knowledge at a point in time. Nearly 150,000 certifications have been issued. ASQ has members in more than 100 countries, in all industries, and in all cultures. ASQ certification is internationally accepted and recognized.

Benefits to the Individual

- New skills gained and proficiency upgraded
- Investment in your career
- Mark of technical excellence
- Assurance that you are current with emerging technologies
- Discriminator in the marketplace
- Certified professionals earn more than their uncertified counterparts
- Certification is endorsed by more than 125 companies

Benefits to the Organization

- Investment in the company's future
- Certified individuals can perfect and share new techniques in the workplace
- Certified staff are knowledgeable and able to assure product and service quality

Quality is a global concept. It spans borders, cultures, and languages. No matter what country your customers live in or what language they speak, they demand quality products and services. You and your organization also benefit from quality tools and practices. Acquire the knowledge to position yourself and your organization ahead of your competition.

Certifications Include

- Biomedical Auditor – CBA
- Calibration Technician – CCT
- HACCP Auditor – CHA
- Pharmaceutical GMP Professional – CPGP
- Quality Inspector – CQI
- Quality Auditor – CQA
- Quality Engineer – CQE
- Quality Improvement Associate – CQIA
- Quality Technician – CQT
- Quality Process Analyst – CQPA
- Reliability Engineer – CRE
- Six Sigma Black Belt – CSSBB
- Six Sigma Green Belt – CSSGB
- Software Quality Engineer – CSQE
- Manager of Quality/Organizational Excellence – CMQ/OE